P9-DML-267

Stuart B. Litvak, Ph.D., Executive Director
of Arizona Counseling and Psychological Services, Phoenix,
has taught psychology/psychotherapy courses
and conducts workshops on stress management, holistic health,
and intellectual enhancement.
He is the author of four books and numerous published articles.

Prentice-Hall International, Inc., London
Prentice-Hall of Australia Pty. Limited, Sydney
Prentice-Hall of Canada, Ltd., Toronto
Prentice-Hall of India Private Limited, New Delhi
Prentice-Hall of Japan, Inc., Tokyo
Prentice-Hall of Southeast Asia Pte. Ltd., Singapore
Whitehall Books Limited, Wellington, New Zealand

USE
YOUR HEAD

*How to Develop
the Other 80% of Your Brain*

STUART B. LITVAK

A SPECTRUM BOOK

Prentice-Hall, Inc., Englewood Cliffs, N.J. 07632

Library of Congress Cataloging in Publication Data

LITVAK, STUART.

  Use your head.

  "A Spectrum Book"
  Includes bibliographical references and index.
   1. Intellect. 2. Intellect–Problems, exercises,
etc. 3. Self-actualization (Psychology) 4. Self-
actualization (Psychology)–Problems, exercises, etc.
I. Title.
BF431.L533   153   81-10694
                         AACR2

ISBN 0-13-939967-4 (PBK.)

ISBN 0-13-939975-5

For Georgia, Michael, Shaina, Z, Madelyn,
and Joseph.

A SPECTRUM BOOK

Printed in the United States of America.

10 9 8 7 6 5 4 3 2 1

Editorial/production supervision by Claudia Citarella
Manufacturing buyer: Cathie Lenard

This Spectrum Book is available to businesses and organizations
at a special discount when ordered in large quantities.
For information, contact Prentice-Hall, Inc.,
General Book Marketing, Special Sales Division,
Englewood Cliffs, N.J. 07632.

CONTENTS

v

When sense has left a head, it should be called a tail.
—Rumi

There are people with dyed hair who fear that it might affect the brain.
But often such people have no brains.
—Proverb

Deep in the sea are riches beyond compare.
But if you seek safely, it is on the shore.
—Saadi

PREFACE

With the tremendous surge of interest in personal development and in increasing one's mental abilities, we find more and more books, articles, and television time devoted to these subjects.

Lately, I have seen several articles in newspapers, tabloids, and magazines advising readers on how to increase their brain power. Usually, eminent psychologists, professors, and brain experts are quoted, and I'm sure many readers try to follow their suggestions. Unfortunately, very little—if any—of the advice given will actually enhance mental abilities or increase brain capacity. The advice given advocates tactics that seem to fall into three general categories: self-hypnosis, physical exercises, and mental exercises.

The *self-hypnosis* method primarily advises people to imagine or suggest to themselves various goals, objectives, or results desired ("My memory is improving daily"). It is basically a combination of positive thinking and wish-fulfillment.

Physical exercises are based on brain research data that correlates various physical activities with correspondent functional areas on the brain. For example, one part of the brain, the cerebellum, is known to assist in the coordination of motor function. Hence, people are advised to engage in activities such as tight-rope walking or typing because these will assist in the development of their cerebellum. Another is holding one's breath as a way of building up the circulatory system of the brain.

The most common advice, however, is that of *mental exercises*. In one recent article, titled "How to Keep Your Mind Young," the experts recommend doing arithmetic problems in one's head, analyzing current events, watching TV quiz shows, doing crossword puzzles, memorizing lists (such as state capitals) and fixing things around the house (like dripping faucets). Another article titled "How to Improve Your Brainpower," suggests keeping one's brain active by trying to solve puzzles, playing games, taking a "course in a subject that challenges you," taking up a new hobby or sport, studying the dictionary to increase one's vocabulary, and so on.

Experts also recommend watching one's nutrition ("eat well-balanced meals"), stop smoking and drinking (smoking affects brain circulation and excessive alcohol slows down nerve functioning), and get lots of physical exercise. "A healthy body and a healthy mind are inseparable."

If you already know how to use your head to some extent, possibly you have already figured out that the usual recommendations for improving brain/mind capacity are actually quite limited, and, in many cases, trite. We use only 20% of our brain. Most of the suggestions offered by the experts will only allow you to get better use of the existing 20% of your brain *you already use*.

In order to use more than 20% of your brain, you need to learn totally new approaches—activities, exercises, experiences, ideas—that *you are not already familiar with*.

This is what this book is all about. It is not a do-this/don't do-that book. Self-help books that specialize in telling you what to do are generally ineffective. In order to make changes in yourself and in your life, you must undergo *new* experiences. This book is carefully designed to assist you in examining your assumptions, your thinking, your perceptions, and your mental habits. Various exercises are provided that will assist in directly provoking your mind and in influencing your general awareness.

Although there is no guarantee or claim that by reading this book you will then be able to use all of your brain, by absorbing the experiences provided, by reading some of the various source books mentioned, and by adapting many of the ideas to your daily life, you should begin to use much more of your brain/mind than only the 20% you now employ.

ACKNOWLEDGMENTS

I wish to thank Nora Burba, whose assistance was invaluable throughout all phases of this book. Thanks too, to Candice Smith for her editing assistance and to Jane Manley for her usual efficiency in proofreading the galleys. Particularly helpful and supportive was my editor at Prentice-Hall, Mary Kennan, her assistant, Stephanie Kiriakopoulos, my production editor, Claudia Citarella, and Ed Ferrang, of course, who mustn't be forgotten, for his "discovery." I am also grateful to Ms. Sharisse Parker for her assistance in procuring the many permissions necessary for the use of copyrighted materials. I owe a great deal of thanks to Mr. Idries Shah, for his generous permission to utilize his materials, which form the basis for this book. Through the years I have been encouraged and assisted by two friends—Messrs. Gary Wieser and Julian DeVries—and although repayment would be impossible, I wish them and theirs the best of everything. Not least, I am greatly appreciative to Kathy "Magic Fingers" Jones who typed the manuscript and its many drafts—with expert speed and precision.

Acknowledgment is gratefully made to the following for permission to reprint excerpts from works published by them:
How to Increase Your Intelligence by W. Wenger, Ph.D., © 1975 by Dell Publishing Company, Inc. Circle-Square Problem by Paul Chance,

"When Rust Clogs Your Brain." Copyright © 1979 by The Condé-Nast Publications Inc. Adaptation of Figure 94 from *Elements of Psychology* by David Krech and Richard S. Crutchfield (New York: Alfred A. Knopf). *Exploring the Crack in the Cosmic Egg* by Joseph Chilton Pearce. © 1974 by Joseph Chilton Pearce. Used by permission of Julian Press, Inc. Excerpt from *Awakening Intuition* by Frances E. Vaughan, © 1979 by Frances E. Vaughan. Reprinted by permission of Doubleday & Company, Inc. and the author. Excerpt from *The Brain: The Last Frontier* by Richard M. Restak, M.D. Copyright © 1979 by Richard M. Restak. Reprinted by permission of Doubleday & Company, Inc. Excerpt from *Person/Planet* by Theodore Roszak. Copyright © 1977, 1978 by Theodore Roszak. Reprinted by permission of Doubleday & Company, Inc. and Victor Gollancz Ltd. Excerpt from *The Right Brain: A New Understanding of the Unconscious Mind and Its Creative Powers* by Thomas Blakeslee, copyright © 1980 by Thomas Blakeslee. Reprinted by permission of Doubleday & Company, Inc. and Macmillan Press Ltd. Quotes and illustration from *Use Both Sides of Your Brain* by Tony Buzan, © 1974 by Tony Buzan. Reprinted by permission of the publisher E.P. Dutton and the British Broadcasting Corp. *The Magical Child*, by Joseph Chilton Pearce, © 1977 by E.P. Dutton Publishing Co., Inc. "An Inquiry into the Persistence of Unwisdom in Government," by Barbara W. Tuchman, *Esquire*, May, 1980. Copyright © 1980 by Barbara W. Tuchman. Reprinted by permission of Russell & Volkening, Inc., as agents for the author. *The Nature of Human Consciousness: A Book of Readings*, edited by Robert E. Ornstein, © 1973 W. H. Freeman and Company Publishers. *In Search of the Miraculous*, G. I. Gurdjieff, quoted by P. D. Ouspensky, © 1949, Harcourt Brace Jovanovich. Reprinted by permission of Harcourt Brace Jovanovich and Routledge & Kegan Paul Ltd. *The Dream Theatre* by Faye Hammel and Daniel Marshall, © 1978, Harper & Row Publishers, Inc. Case 17 "Mrs. Allen of Vaughan Road" (p. 37) from *Incredible Coincidence*, by Alan Vaughan (J. B. Lippincott). Copyright © 1979 by Alan Vaughan. Reprinted by permission of Harper & Row, Publishers, Inc. and Michael Larsen/Elizabeth Pomada Literary Agents. Specified excerpt from page 29 and "Circle Exercise" (p. 184) in *Lateral Thinking: Creativity Step by Step* by Edward de Bono. © 1970 by Edward de Bono. Reprinted by permission of Harper & Row, Publishers, Inc. and Ward Lock Educational Limited. Excerpt from

p. xv in *The Macroscope: A New World Scientific System* by Joël de Rosnay. English translation © 1979 by Harper & Row, Publishers, Inc. Reprinted by permission of Harper & Row, Publishers, Inc. and Editions du Seuil. *Mindways: A Guide for Exploring Your Mind* by Louis M. Savary and Margaret Ehlen-Miller © 1979, Harper & Row, Publishers, Inc. *The Paranormal* by Stan Gooch, © 1978 by Harper & Row, Publishers, Inc. "Dirty Words" (pp. 91, 195) in *Rival Hypotheses: Alternative Interpretations of Data Based Conclusions* by Schuyler W. Huck and Howard M. Sandler, © 1979 by Schuyler W. Huck and Howard M. Sandler. Reprinted by permission of Harper & Row, Publishers, Inc. Excerpt from (p. 69) *Transpersonal Psychologies*, edited by Charles T. Tart. Copyright © 1975 by Harper & Row, Publishers, Inc. Reprinted by permission of Harper & Row, Publishers, Inc. *The Luck Factor* by Max Gunther © 1977 by Max Gunther. Reprinted by permission of Macmillan Publishing Co., Inc. Tass news release and statement by Lyndon B. Johnson in *Mother Jones*, © 1980, *Mother Jones*. Quote in *New Realities* (Vol. III, No. 3) by Richard Bach, © 1980 by *New Realities*, 680 Beach Street, San Francisco, Ca. 94109. "Machines that Think," *Newsweek*, June 30 1980, © 1980 by Newsweek, Inc. All rights reserved. Reprinted by permission. "Best Sellers," by Andy Meisler, © 1980 by the New York Magazine Company, Inc. Reprinted with the permission of New West magazine. "A Letter From the Director," *Human Nature*, January 1979, by Dr. Robert Ornstein, © 1980 Dr. Robert Ornstein. "The Split and the Whole Brain," *Human Nature*, May 1978, © 1978 by Dr. Robert Ornstein. *A New Model of the Universe* by P. D. Ouspensky, Kegan Paul Ltd., London, 1931, pp. 295–296. Vintage Books, New York, 1971, pp. 263–264. Reprinted by permission of the estate of Peter D. Ouspensky. Problems and answers are reprinted by permission of Perigee Books from *Creative Growth Games* by Eugene Raudsepp and George P. Hough, Jr. Copyright © 1977 by Eugene Raudsepp and George P. Hough, Jr. *The Money Personality* by Sidney Lecker. Copyright © 1979 by Sidney Lecker. Reprinted by permission of Simon & Schuster, a Division of Gulf & Western Corporation. *PO: A Device for Successful Thinking* by Edward de Bono. Copyright © 1972 by European Services Ltd. Reprinted by permission of Simon & Schuster, a Division of Gulf & Western Corporation and A. P. Watt Ltd. *The Act of Creation* by Arthur Koestler. Copyright © 1964 by Arthur Koestler. Reprinted by permission of The Sterling Lord

Agency, Inc. and A D Peters & Co. Ltd. *New Pathways in Psychology: Maslow & the Post-Freudian Revolution* by Colin Wilson (Taplinger, 1972). © 1972 by Colin Wilson. Reprinted by permission of Taplinger Publishing Co., Inc. and Bolt & Watson Ltd. *Drawing on the Right Side of the Brain* by Betty Edwards, 1979, J. P. Tarcher. *The Aquarian Conspiracy* by Marilyn Ferguson, 1980 J. P. Tarcher/ Houghton Mifflin Company. *Common Knowledge* by Robert Ornstein, 1975 Viking/Compass. Excerpts from *The Mind Field* by Robert Ornstein. Copyright © 1976 by Robert Ornstein. Reprinted by permission of Viking Penguin Inc. *The Secret Garden*, Octagon Press, London, 1969. The introduction by el-Quadiri is also reprinted in *The Elephant in the Dark*, Leonard Lewin, ed., Dutton, 1972, pp. 137-43. Quote by Karl Pribrum, *Snapping: America's Epidemic of Sudden Personality Change*, Flo Conway and Jim Siegelman, Delta, 1978, pp. 121-24. An adapted version of two illustrations (p. 85) from *The Book of Think: Or, How to Solve Problems Twice Your Size* by Marilyn Burns, illustrated by Martha Weston. © 1976 by The Yolla Bolly Press. Used by permission of Little, Brown and Company. The article from "Machine Candidate," Diane K. Shah with Richard Manning, *Newsweek*, August 20, 1980. *The Crack in the Cosmic Egg* by Joseph Chilton Pearce. Copyright © 1971 by Joseph Chilton Pearce. By permission of Julian Press, Inc. The following extracts are reprinted with permission from A. P. Watt Ltd. and Idries Shah: *The Exploits of the Incomparable Mulla Nasrudin*, © 1966 by Mulla Nasrudin Enterprises Ltd.; *The Pleasantries of the Incredible Mulla Nasrudin*, © 1968 by Mulla Nasrudin Enterprises Ltd.; *Tales of the Dervishes*, © 1967 by Idries Shah; *The Way of the Sufi*, © 1968 by Idries Shah; *Reflections*, © 1971 by Idries Shah; *Perfumed Scorpion*, © 1978 by Idries Shah; *Caravan of Dreams*, © 1968 by Idries Shah; *The Magic Monastery*, © 1972 by Idries Shah; *The Wisdom of the Idiots*, © 1969 by Idries Shah; *The Sufis*, © 1964 by Idries Shah; *Special Illuminations*, © 1977 by Idries Shah; *World Tales*, © 1979 by Idries Shah. The two illustrations, "The Unsuspected Element" and "The Short Cut," illustrated by Richard Williams from *The Exploits of the Incomparable Mulla Nasrudin* by Idries Shah are reprinted by permission of the author, illustrator, and Jonathan Cape Limited. © 1966 Mulla Nasrudin Enterprises Limited.

chapter one
THE UNLIMITED BRAIN

There are souls who are born in bustling metropoli such as Toad Suck, Arkansas or Tuba City, Arizona, spend their entire adult lives there, then are gently laid to rest beneath their native dirt without ever having seen the lights of Paris—or Peoria, for that matter. So comfortable and familiar are they in their own little acres that they seldom wish to push themselves past their city limits into the world beyond.

The part of the mind that we use is sort of like living in Toad Suck or Tuba City. We are familiar and comfortable with what we know and seldom wish to push ourselves further. Yet the brain is a vast universe, one which is as extensive and overwhelming as the infinite cosmos. But we tend to occupy only a small part of that entire cerebral universe.

Recent research about the brain and mind leads us to conclude:

> What we *are* gathering from our efforts at the moment is a knowledge that the mind is infinitely more subtle than we previously thought, and that everyone who has what is ironically called a 'normal' mind has a much larger ability and potential than was previously thought.[1]

[1]Tony Buzan, *Use Both Sides of Your Brain* (New York: Dutton, 1976), p. 13.

What sort of research allows us to arrive at this conclusion? There are several such lines of research, drawn from an understanding of neurophysiology, transpersonal psychology, hypnosis, brain chemistry, studies of creativity, infotronics, holographic technology, and our ancient lore of Eastern teachings. Here then, in a brain cell (so to speak), some of the more salient findings are summarized.

NEUROPHYSIOLOGY   Studies reveal there are ten to fifteen billion nerve cells (neurons) in the human brain. As a result, the possibilities are practically infinite. Although there are an estimated 10^{100} atoms in the entire universe, *one* brain, with ten billion neurons has a potential for 10^{800} interconnections. Put another way,

> ... Dr. Kenneth Boulding, President of the American Association for the Advancement of Science, estimates that the capacity of the human brain is 'literally inconceivably large.' If each of the brain's fifteen billion neurons is capable of only two states (on or off), the capacity would be 2^{10} billionth power. To write out this number at the rate of one digit per second would take ninety years, or about the projected human lifespan in the twenty-first century. In comparison, the number of neutrinos (about the smallest particle in existence) that could be packed into the total astronomical universe ten billion light years across, could be written down in four minutes.[2]

TRANSPERSONAL PSYCHOLOGY   A new branch of modern psychology, the perspective of transpersonal psychology, is understanding extended awareness and higher conscious development. Its unofficial founder is Dr. Abraham Maslow, known for his studies of "self-actualized" or exceptional people. Breaking with psychological tradition and its emphasis on illness, Maslow studied the healthy qualities of humans, especially why some excelled in their fields and others didn't. Maslow's theory is that there are five ascending levels of human needs (physiological, safety, love, esteem, and self-actualization) and as one need level becomes satisfied, the next takes over. In his studies, he discovered, however, that most people reach only the level of self-esteem, with a rare minority becoming self-actualized. People he considered as

[2]Richard Restak, *The Brain: The Last Frontier* (New York: Doubleday, 1979), pp. 159–60.

self-actualizers included many outstanding creative personalities, such as Haydn, Goethe, Franklin, Whitman, and others. He concluded that almost everyone comes into the world with the capacity to self-actualize but that few do so because most people become socially conditioned to the "Jonah complex:"

> One day, he [Maslow] asked his students: 'Which of you expects to achieve greatness in your chosen field?' The class looked at him blankly. After a long silence, Maslow said: 'If not you—who then?' And they began to see his point. This is the fallacy of insignificance, the certainty that you are unlucky and unimportant, the Jonah complex.[3]

Associated with being a self-actualizer, Maslow found that these exceptional people reported (more so than others) having had *peak-experiences:* "mystic experiences, moments of great awe, moments of the most intense happiness, or even rapture, ecstasy or bliss..."

HYPNOSIS   Studies with hypnosis during the past hundred years have yielded at least two general findings that are significant in understanding human potential: (1) evidence that the unconscious mind exists and (2) that numerous abilities can be displayed under hypnosis but not necessarily in normal waking life. Under hypnosis (or post-hypnotically) people may reveal greater self-confidence, greater physical strength, feats of memory, creative imagination, and most importantly, talents they normally do not display. These are usually creative talents such as the ability to act, imitate others, paint, dance and sing, or expressive talents, such as the ability to behave more maturely, to act boldly and without hesitation, and to be joyful. Although these people tend to not display these talents normally, it is exceedingly interesting to note that hypnosis did not *add* anything to their preexistent repertoire; it merely provided them with the *belief* that they could do so.

BRAIN CHEMISTRY   One scientist, Dr. David Samuels of the Weizmann Institute, estimates that in the average brain there are between 100,000 and 1,000,000 *different* chemicals reacting. Studies

[3]Colin Wilson, *New Pathways in Psychology* (New York: Taplinger Publishing Co., 1972), p. 1.

on the use of psychopharmaceuticals (mind-altering drugs) reveal that the brain/mind is capable of a wide spectrum of altered states of consciousness—many of which are suprasensory, transcendent, and rapturous in nature. These are the commonly reported experiences with such drugs as LSD, cocaine, mescaline, marijuana, and others. What is significant about this is that the drug itself does not produce the actual experience; the drug is merely a stimulus or a catalyst that sets off a chain of reactions among biochemicals that are *already there* in the brain. Because drugs do have numerous drawbacks—side effects, sometimes negative experiences, ease of abuse, and mainly their temporary effects—our knowledge of such drugs does nonetheless provide us with firsthand evidence that higher, more expansive experiences are indeed possible. The potential is always there. Optimally, we should be able to learn to start this chain of chemical reactions naturally, without reaching for the stash bag or the medicine chest.

CREATIVITY STUDIES   Many studies have revealed that man's potential for creativity is there. It simply needs encouragement and proper orientation.

In Berkeley, California, for instance, the Carnegie Institute has pioneered a program for developing a kind of free intuitive creativity in young children. The young child is presented with problem-filled adventure readings, situations without formal, logical conclusions, where no prestructured logical "answer" exists, even in the minds of the creators of the system. The child has to create a "solution" freely in order to continue the adventure, and the self-motivated technique avoids those arbitrary absolutes which act as constricting, goal-oriented motivations in ordinary education. With no a priori answer, and no outside criteria, the child develops a trust and confidence in an inner, open logic too often stifled by formal schooling. Developing this free-synthesis capacity has led, in turn, to impressive leaps of the intelligence quotient itself—that questionable gauge of reality-thinking.

The whole experiment is a gesture toward bridging the modes of mind, and the results could reach beyond science fiction. We may yet see the day when the tragedy of school is overcome.[4]

[4]Joseph Chilton Pearce, *The Crack in the Cosmic Egg* (New York: Simon & Schuster/Pocket Books, 1973), p. 187.

In another example, recent studies by Dr. Betty Edwards (discussed in greater detail later in this book) have revealed that virtually anyone, with the assistance of a new kind of training designed to develop the "right brain," can become proficient in painting and drawing in only thirty to sixty days.

Infotronics, a term coined by Karl Albrecht,[5] is the name given to the rapidly growing field of integrated-circuit microprocessor electronics, which is becoming the basis for remarkable studies in computer technology. Advanced computers and ingenious programs are now revealing much about the vast capacities of human intelligence and brain function. In an article titled "Machines That Think" (*Newsweek*, June 30, 1980), the following was included in answer to the question posed to the experts: "How Smart Can Computers Get?":

> ... machine consciousness might be achieved once the programmers get a computer to think about thinking and to understand its own process of understanding ... But even if silicon sensibilities never love, grieve or fear, intelligent computers have already changed man's sense of himself as the only thinking being. Humanity has survived other jolts to its ego, from Copernicus to Darwin, and it will undoubtedly survive this one, too.

But infotronics only makes it that much more clear that the human brain has extensive capacities beyond those normally tapped. Even with our present knowledge about computers, if we were to construct one computer to match the capacity of the human brain, experts surmise that the computer hardware would cover an area equal to that of the state of California, and the energy required to run it would generate enough heat to warm the oceans and significantly alter the temperature balance of the world.

HOLOGRAPHIC TECHNOLOGY   Brain researchers are now starting to consider the brain as a *hologram*. A hologram is a new form of photography that contains the entire photograph within any part or section of the whole, and that yields a very real, 3-D effect. For example, if you take a holographic plate showing a

[5]Karl Albrecht, *Brain Power* (Englewood Cliffs, NJ: Prentice-Hall, 1980), pp. 285–87.

picture of a table and break it into smaller pieces, one piece doesn't show a part of the table, but the whole table. Researchers and psychologists have considered the hologram as a model of the brain, maintaining that the brain works as a whole—that sections of the brain, even an individual cell, may reflect the workings of the entire brain. Further, these theorists believe the brain may be a hologram of the entire earth or universe, and that the "human brain may be a kind of microminiature replica of the living planet itself, just rather fuzzy at the edges, needing clarification." The point for our consideration is that,

> At birth, the brain, as a hologram fragment, must have exposure to and interact with the earth hologram to achieve clarity, to bring the brain's picture into focus, so to speak. Confine a newly-born brain and prevent interaction with the earth, and no clarification takes place ... the larger and more elaborate the brain, the wider the hologram effect of that species and the greater its intelligence or ability to interact.[6]

One psychologist, Karl Pribrum, has taken the hologram/ brain idea one step further, and speculates that,

> Now if the hologram is something that is for real in the brain ... it means that we can store things in our brains in terms of various frequencies of information. Then we read out the information in either linear or spatial fashion. The linear way is sequential, over time, and the spatial is simultaneous. Space and time are not *in* the brain; they are *read out* of it ... every part of the hologram ... includes everything. All the information is there, from a slightly different window or viewpoint. Nonetheless, each part represents the whole, and that, of course, is Godlike, isn't it? ...
>
> The holographic notion applies to all of the spiritual ideas we've ever had ... but it also applies to everything we know about social organization ...
>
> I think the hologram notion is in fact a real change in our scientific paradigm. It makes studiable by scientific tools all the things that have been dismissed as mystical and subjective and so on. In other words, here is an explanatory device that turns the corner.[7]

[6]Joseph Chilton Pearce, *The Magical Child* (New York: Dutton, 1977), pp. 6–8.
[7]Flo Conway and Jim Siegelman, *Snapping: America's Epidemic of Sudden Personality Change* (New York: Delta Publishing, 1978), pp. 121–24.

If the brain/hologram idea is accepted, even in theory, it does suggest the view that our brain is much more versatile than we think it is and surely contains possibilities that are far beyond normal expectations.

ANCIENT EASTERN TEACHINGS   All the great Eastern schools of thought, many alive and active to this day, share the claim that humans can develop far beyond their usual (self-imposed) limitations. And these claims take us much further than those implied by Maslow. Yoga, Buddhism, Zen, Hinduism, Taoism, Sufism, Jewish Cabbalism, Christian Mysticism, and the other spiritual/psychological systems for centuries have made higher human development their specialization. The teacher-disciple relationship is as old as civilization itself, and with proper knowledge (to which these systems hold claim), through what has been described as a "science of man," the human mind can develop to levels undreampt of. These claims are easily substantiated with the developed sage as their product and proof. For example, in the Sufi tradition, some of the greatest saints of all time have emerged, such as Jalaludin Rumi (thirteenth-century revered teacher and author of *The Musnavi*), Omar Khayyam (*The Rubaiyat*), Imam El-Ghazali (The "Proof of Islam"), Sheikh Saadi of Shiraz (thirteenth-century classical author) and many others up to the present day, most of whom remain anonymous. The point is that almost anyone—in any culture—with proper orientation and preparation has the latent capacity to develop far beyond the norm.

Even though the researchers will insist that their method—the neurophysiology, the transpersonal psychology, or whatever—is the best way to expand the mind's potential, each of these lines of research have one thing in common: they are our one-way tickets out of our mental Toad Sucks and Tuba Cities.

Just for a while, then, forget the "city limits" on your mind and consider the many possibilities discussed in this chapter. Attempt to keep an open mind with this book as you explore your mental world beyond.

chapter two
THE "FIFTH" EXPERIENCE

It's hard to imagine the mind having so much unlimited potential, particularly when you are faced with mind-boggling feats like remembering how to change the tire on your car, figuring out why you're overdrawn at the bank, or coming up with something clever to say on a thank-you note.

Part of the answer to this eternal dilemma lies in our understanding of how the mind/brain works. The brain, like the old nag who only knows the way back to the barn, is habit-bound. It is a pattern-making system that works on the principle of least resistance, relying on patterns formed early in life, disregarding information that does not seem useful for survival.

Skeptical? Look at the three triangles in Figure 2–1 and read the caption in each very quickly.[1]

Figure 2–1.

[1]M. L. J. Abercrombie, *The Anatomy of Judgement* (London: Hutchinson, 1969); quoted in Albert Low, *Zen and Creative Management* (New York: Doubleday/Anchor, 1976), p. 164.

Next, read the sentence in Figure 2–2 carefully. How many times does the letter *f* appear? Count them once and only once.

FINISHED FILES ARE THE RE-
SULT OF YEARS OF SCIENTIF-
IC STUDY COMBINED WITH THE
EXPERIENCE OF MANY YEARS.

Figure 2–2.

Aha! Probably fooled you. If you are not yet convinced your brain is habitbound and tends to form patterns, then look again at the three triangles. Did you notice that a word was duplicated in each triangle? What about the *f*s? Did you count six? Because the *f* in *of* is pronounced "vee," we tend to overlook it. The habitual brain, then, tends to see what it expects, not necessarily what is, much like infatuation.

The key to understanding how our brain sets up patterns is found deep within our memory banks. A memory is anything that happens that does not completely "unhappen." The result? A trace is left, which can last only moments—or forever. "I can't seem to forget you, your cheap perfume stays on my clothes." Information that comes into the brain leaves a trace, or alters the surface of the nerve cells that form the memory surface. It's sort of like a landscape.

> A landscape is a memory surface. The contours of a surface offer an accumulated memory trace of the water that has fallen upon it. The rainfall forms little rivulets which combine into streams and then into rivers. Once the pattern of drainage has been formed, then it tends to become ever more permanent since the rain is collected into the drainage channels and tends to make them deeper. It is the rainfall that is doing the sculpting and yet it is the response of the surface to the rainfall that is organizing how the rainfall will do its sculpting.[2]

The recording surface in the brain isn't soil and rocks that give way to the forces of wind and water; it's a network of

[2]Edward de Bono, *Lateral Thinking* (New York: Harper & Row, Pub./Colophon, 1970), p. 29.

interconnected nerve fibers that give way to the forces of experience. Brain patterns are common or familiar experiences that tend
to produce established pathways, which work to assimilate or fit in
new information.

Like a design on fabric or wallpaper, brain patterns tend to
repeat themselves, so that seeing part of the design will lead up to
predictable expectations about the remainder. Hence, a pattern is
anything where items of information interrelate in a predictable
fashion producing an expectancy. In regard to the mind, such
expectancies are commonly referred to as predispositions, preconceptions, or mental sets. These expectancies are useful in a
repeatable, familiar situation (who has time to spend hours analyzing the *best* way to comb your hair??), however, these same
expectancies can become a hindrance when one is faced with
unfamiliar situations or new problems.

If you'd like to see just how much we depend on these little
mental predispositions, try this exercise:

Examine the following sequence of numbers and try to
determine the basis for their progression.

8 1 6 4 3 7 0 1 2

Whether or not you succeeded, try the following exercise. Where
does the Z go: above or below the line, and why?

A		EF	HI	KLMN		T	VWXY
	BCD	G	J		OPQRS	U	

Most mortals attempt to determine the solution to the first exercise
by using mathmetics because this is their "mind set" or "pre-
disposition" based upon familiar experience. However, the numer-
ical sequence is based on the shape of the numbers—every other
number has a curve in it. Now look again at the Z problem and see
if you can determine the solution.

Pattern thinking, then, is far more prevalent than we realize.
Every culture has its patterns engraved in its inhabitants almost
from birth; they shape thinking and experience in a highly
predictable fashion. These patterns are programmed into us so

completely that we tend to exhibit a bit of robotlike behavior. That's why it's been so easy for scientists to design computers that can imitate us. Frightening, isn't it?

A good example of how we tend to think in patterns is provided in the Figure 2–3 (*Newsweek*, August 20, 1979) on page 12.

Those three "dramatic views of the world"—cold war, neo-isolationist and power-politics—described in the article are most revealing. It probably never occurred to any of the people polled that there is any other way of considering such matters. Such is the power of mind sets.

FREEDOM

'I always looked at the alternatives,' said the sheep; 'I can munch or I can bite.'[3]

Let's apply these mind sets to a larger situation—the problems of the world. Are there alternatives in certain tense situations? Of course; in fact there are many. But the strength of our thinking patterns is extreme—we need special effort to realize the alternatives. Consider the Panama Canal, an issue that is still raging at home. Rather than the usual approaches that have been considered, we could, for example, use an *internationalist* alternative, one in which neither the U.S. nor the Panama would control the canal. All countries (or the United Nations) could use the canal as a means to encourage world-wide cooperation and peace.

A more chilling example of the operation of mental patterns is provided by Yale University's Artificial Intelligence labs in which "...the prospect of a thinking computer has progressed from the realm of science to imminent reality. Some people are now claiming that the human brain's performance may soon be duplicated by tiny blinking lights, spinning discs and a labyrinth of cables." At Yale, Drs. Roger Schank and Christopher Riesbeck have devised programs that actually allow computers to carry on "live" conversations with humans. The computer is so convincing, that most people can't tell it isn't human. This is made possible because Schank and Riesbeck have discovered that people think and talk

[3]Idries Shah, "Freedom," *Reflections* (New York: Viking/Penguin, 1972), p. 15.

MACHINE CANDIDATE

IDEAS

NEWSWEEK

"First of all," intones the speaker, "let me say that the United States is not a failure. I recognize that it's foolhardy to unilaterally disarm, but . . ." So begins an upbeat, let's-look-at-the-record foreign-policy speech that could well be the kickoff of the 1980 primaries. The speaker, however, is not Jimmy Carter, Ted Kennedy or even Howard Baker, but a fresh political voice from the Midwest. The name? IBM-370.

The slick-tongued computer-orator is the brainchild of two communications professors who believe that getting elected to

Jeff Lowenthal—NEWSWEEK

Cragan and computer: 'My fellow Americans . . . '

public office is becoming more a matter of manipulating campaign symbols than dealing with substance. To prove their thesis, they set out to program the IBM-370 to write the "perfect" foreign-policy speech—one guaranteed, that is, to appeal to the most and offend the fewest in any given audience. "We figured that if we did the proper market-type research and programed the computer to write a speech reflecting the findings, the speech would end up sounding pretty much like the genuine article churned out by a pack of poll-watching speechwriters," says John Cragan of Illinois State University.

'DRAMA': To begin with, Cragan, 35, and partner Donald Shields, 34, of the University of Missouri-St. Louis, theorized that all a politician need do to get elected is recognize that voters generally subscribe to one of three "dramatic" views of the world, then play to the most widespread of the views. Set in a foreign-policy context, these three attitudes translated into cold-war, neo-isolationist and power-politics mind-sets. On the Panama Canal, for instance, the cold-war view held that the U.S. ought not to surrender the Canal Zone, the neo-isolationist view dictated that the U.S. get out of Panama and the power-politics view supported the negotiation of a new treaty to protect U.S. interests in the zone.

The professors picked twenty such issues to be covered by the speech. They culled newspapers and magazines for months, jotting down quotes that reflected all three positions on all twenty issues, then transferred the quotes onto 60 index cards. Finally, they went to—where else?—Peoria, Ill., to see how the opinions played. Sixty Peorians were asked to sort the cards in order of preference, from those most reflective of their views to those least reflective. Then the subjects rearranged the cards to show how important each issue was to them.

1984-ISH: Cragan and Shields fed the results into the computer and instructed it to write a speech based on the most prevalent opinions, complete with adverbs and adjectives. They pushed a button and out came the hypothetical candidate's carefully considered opinion on how best to handle U.S. foreign policy—for Peorians. "The point," says Cragan, "is that you can take any idiot, parade him around the country for twelve months, and get him elected."

But the ultimate purpose behind this slightly 1984-ish project, say the two professors, is to force politicians out of the business of manipulating symbols and back into the business of governing. To that end, their IBM-370 is about to churn out perfect speeches on energy, foreign policy and domestic policy. "When we publish these speeches in 1980," says Cragan, "we hope it will spark enough controversy for someone to ask the candidates why their speeches sound so much like our computer's. Maybe that will get them to say what they really think for a change."

So far, that message hasn't got through. Instead of coming clean, six political aspirants, including a candidate in a gubernatorial primary and a mayoral contender, have already called on Cragan and Shields for a little help from their computer. All were turned down—and lost their races.

DIANE K. SHAH with
RICHARD MANNING in Chicago

Figure 2–3.

according to *scripts*: "The script is a structure that describes the appropriate sequence of events in a particular context. Scripts handle and stylize everyday situations. It's a predetermined, stereotyped sequence of actions that defines a well-known situation."[4]

Think about all the scripts you rely on as the movie reel of life rolls along. Scripts you use in situations like first dates, visiting the dentist, being in a library, eating at a swanky restaurant—it's a matter of knowing your lines and expecting certain responses. When someone ad libs, it throws you. Schank's and Riesbeck's computer is successful, then, because they have realized that there are a limited and finite amount of standard thinking/acting/speaking patterns that control the human in any typical situation.

Our "current" way of looking at things is what is meant by the "fifth" experience: that we prefer to use 20% of our brain—over and over again. If we are going to start getting more from our brain, we must first recognize our condition, and become conscious of our thinking patterns, mind sets, and "scripts." By becoming aware of the operation of these processes within us, we are at least on our way to examining new possibilities and exercising options which were formerly hidden from view and hence, for all intents, totally unavailable to us.

[4]Richard Restak, *The Brain: The Last Frontier* (New York: Doubleday, 1979), p. 339.

chapter three
REALITY BY CONSENSUS

We say "nice to meet you" when we are introduced to someone new. We are (usually) faithful to our mates. Our children attend school during their early years. We try to make as much money as we can. We keep our bodily functions private. These are some of the subtle "rules" we live by. There are a myriad of them controlling everything from the kind of hairstyle we wear to the manner in which we think. It's known as *conditioning*, and like the goo our hairdressers use, it's used as a tool to keep our psychological, cultural, and societal selves tangle-free and healthy.

Although thinkers have been aware of conditioning for many centuries, it's only been in the last sixty years that psychologists and social scientists have taken the topic seriously and have attempted to study it. But even psychologists have been unable to understand conditioning beyond what they observe and describe in their animal and human subjects. It's the old that's-easy-for-you-to-say syndrome. Like the other members of their culture, their own conditioning escapes them.

In describing his fellow sociologists (and himself), Dr. Harold Garfinkle noted that they "are like goldfish swimming in a bowl, confidently analyzing other goldfish without ever having discovered the bowl or the water they have in common with the fish they are studying."[1] Not to mention their scales and fins.

[1] Tim Tyler, "The Ethnomethodologist," *Human Behavior* (April 1974), p. 58.

14

We are all goldfish, looking for crumbs of food, swimming about in the waters of conditioning that penetrate our every cell. Few of us ever realize that what we call our opinions or beliefs are really not our own, but those ever-so-subtly implanted by others and by social and cultural institutions.

This is not to imply that conditioning is all bad; on the contrary, a good portion of it is very essential. Getting back to the hairdresser analogy, it gets us through some potential snarls and aids us in getting along with our neighbors next door. After all, we wouldn't know how to do many basic sorts of activities if it weren't for conditioning or training: bladder control, reading, writing, computation, good manners, cheating on our tax returns, and the like. In effect, we are given certain advantages by our conditioning—yet at the same time, certain disadvantages. It is the disadvantages which concern us here; simply because we are victims of a process that has greatly restricted our view of reality and fuller use of our minds.

Ordinary consciousness—the kind we usually put on right after we shower in the morning—is simply the state of mind we experience as the result of lifelong conditioning or indoctrination. Practically all persons in a culture who consider themselves normal or rational share a reality that is true by agreement; in other words a consensus reality. This consensus reality dictates our most basic processes: what we think, our experience, what we sense in our environment, and, of course, how we behave. These processes are so much a part of our daily functioning that we rarely notice them and almost never question it (can you imagine how difficult it would be to get going in the morning if you had to question *why* you had to get out of bed, *why* a shower would help you to wake up, *why* you had to be at work or school by a reasonable time?).

Because this consensus reality process is so subtle, we don't pay much attention to it while functioning within our own culture. It can, however, become clearer if we visit another culture (ever notice how people tend to behave differently for a while after they've come back from a prolonged visit to another country?). For example, we in North America take it for granted that being punctual for an appointment is important (we are a Type A society, after all). But in Latin America or in the Middle East, however, this is not necessarily the case. Many North Americans, entrenched in the Puritan work ethic, find it extremely difficult to adjust to these cultures. For example, in these other countries, government officials or businessmen may have a large reception area outside their private office in which people can come and go throughout the day. If several people arrive at once, they might assemble in different areas of the reception room, and the person they are visiting may move about the room conferring with each. Waiting hours to see someone is not that unusual. People in those countries can be extremely patient.

As bizarre as this situation may seem to us, it is perfectly natural to Latin Americans and Middle Easterners. On the other hand, should they visit our culture, punctuality, appointment books, and time-restricted activities that seem natural to us, may appear extremely strange to them—even crazy.

Essentially, we all come into this world with a plethora of potentialities. But depending on the culture we are in, some of these traits are considered good and encouraged, while others are suppressed. What any particular culture deems important or valuable is accomplished through the mechanism of selectivity.

In Western culture—particularly in the United States—a great emphasis is placed upon making money—the more money, the merrier. As a result, many people devote their entire life to this goal, becoming money-making machines. They have dollar signs in their pupils. Family, love, relaxation, and education become secondary. Maybe this is an extreme example, but it illustrates how certain values, when pursued, blind us to other possibilities and realities. To a money-making "robot," a tree is not considered a beautiful part of nature that casts an inviting bit of shade on a hot summer afternoon; it becomes paper or lumber. $$. A house may not be a sanctuary; it becomes a great, inexpensive place to set up an office.

Realizing that this kind of conditioning operates to stifle many of our potential abilities and blinds us to many aspects of reality, the question becomes: How do we break free of its hold? Some gloom-and-doom thinkers and writers believe that there is no way to break free. This is the existentialist or pessimistic point of view. However, not everyone is obligated to accept this view, and intimations of possibilities may be found in the rich heritage of the East.

Borrowing from both ancient and contemporary sources, certain general guidelines suggest themselves. These guidelines do not guarantee you will escape your conditioning, but they will sensitize you to some possibilities and will allow you to prepare should you discover a "way" that better suits you and your real needs.

1. *Questioning Values.* Is money that important to you? A trendy condo with the "right" address necessary for your happiness? Consider all of the values deemed important by your culture and whether these need to be important for you also. Read, explore, and do research into other cultural values and honestly try to ask yourself what would suit you and your particular inner makeup. For example, instead of a materialistic, product-orientated, consuming lifestyle, would you find greater satisfaction from more internal, spiritual and growth-oriented values? Or would you wish to blend the two?

2. *Nonattachment.* Pretend you are a Betamax and record yourself occasionally, then play yourself back, grab some popcorn, and observe. In other words, learn to stand back, to disassociate yourself from your everyday activities and train yourself to observe yourself and question your doings ("Why do I keep watching TV when there are better things to do?"). Where are you headed? How are you or others around you benefitting from your particular lifestyle?

3. *Qualities.* Do you love to be the center of attention? Hate to share good fortune with others? Use people to get ahead without giving them anything in return? Get irritated when someone asks you to explain something in detail? As you may have surmised, everyone has his or her share of negative or destructive qualities in addition to their positive traits. Many of these negative features we share with our four-footed companions: greed, selfishness, jealousy, narcissism, temper, laziness, impatience, and prejudice. Negative qualities such as these enslave us. The first step to freedom is to recognize and admit these negative tendencies in ourselves and either change them or neutralize them.

4. *Travel.* In Moscow, you stand in line for *everything*. In Paris, as well as among cultivated Americans, cutting your salad with a knife is disgusting. In London, civilization still revolves around tea-time. As mentioned earlier, exposure to other cultures can be quite enlightening (although for some it's an economic difficulty). Travel allows us insight into our subtle, cultural proclivities and permits us an opportunity to consider alternatives. Spending time with a foreign person or ethnic subculture is another way of getting a bit of this type of input.

5. *Nonconformity.* Most of us know an eccentric or a nonconformist who carries his worldly belongings in a box on his head or who shaves his hair off and wears day-glo sheets while chanting "baba au rhum" on the streetcorners. Maybe these individualists irritate you, but you've got to hand it to them—the pressures to conform in any society are extremely strong and are difficult to resist. It's easier to be like the rest than to blaze new trails. This refers not only to outward behavior but to thinking as well. It is much less serious to conform outwardly than inwardly. Learn to question your opinions, beliefs, and culturally shared obsessions. What your culture considers important may or may not be what you truly think is important.

6. *Tolerance.* "You vill read zis and you vill *enjoy* zis. . . ." Dogmatism is a way of imposing restrictions upon the freedom of others, but most importantly, on ourselves. Think about it. Just try to name one aspect of life for which there is only one viewpoint, only one way of doing something. Be honest. In everything from career choices to cleaning the bathtub, there is a multiplicity of options and beliefs. Most events that happen to us can be interpreted in more than one way. It's interesting how often we will instantly jump to conclusions and assume only one, single interpretation. Look at it this way—a glass can be half full or half empty; a "no" can mean a "yes;" a misfortune can be a blessing in disguise. By becoming sensitized to the subtle process of interpretation, we can relieve ourselves of self-imposed restrictions and perceptual myopia.

7. *Challenging Institutions.* Ever notice how we tend to take any news given to us by the networks as gospel? For instance, when doctors tell us that smoking is the leading cause of lung cancer, we never even question it? Not that doctors and the network news

organizations are wrong or are lying, but they represent major institutions and their power over us is strong. Medicine, religion, the media, government, education, and business are the six major institutions in any given modern culture; they are the bulwark of society and function together to establish the norm. They are our official leading source of control, indoctrination, and conditioning. "The Establishment" was the epithet hurled at members of these institutions during the flamboyant sixties. However, today people are becoming more sensitized to the power of this establishment, and many are beginning to question its control over our lives.

8. *Nonexpectancy.* Many of us *expect* to be married someday and to produce a small brood of grinning children. Many of us *expect* to rise to the top of the corporate ladder and work in lavish offices high above the city. Expectations, however, continually produce a hidden control over our minds and perceptions. We often miss many interesting alternatives because we are so intent on meeting our expectations within a certain time period. By suspending our expectations (without eliminating aspirations), we can increase our objectivity in situations and minimize unwarranted disappointments.

9. *Breaking Addictions.* The only way Jane Doe will be happy is if she has a new Mercedes every other year. John Deer will not be satisfied unless he makes at least $50,000 a year. Bob Buck just *has* to watch Monday night football. An addiction is not something that occurs only with cigarettes, alcohol, or drugs. It comes in many forms, like material possessions, money, sports, food, music, the desire for attention, sleep, television, dependency on others and so forth. In order to begin to be free, it helps to become aware of our addictions, and to aim at weaning ourselves from their power.

10. *Pattern Busting.* Try to realize that, for most of us, our daily lives run in patterns—routines which are repeated day after day. By becoming accustomed to these routines, we become like machines. But this robot-existence, this mechanicalness, blinds us to other possibilities. In effect, we rarely question the *quality* of our life. Instead, we unconsciously fight our prison existence by escapes, such as TV, alcohol, drugs, fantasy, novels, movies, diversions, "causes," holidays, games, sexual excess, sleep, and so on. But, as S.J. Lec (*New Unkempt Thoughts*) notes, "Now that you have broken through the wall with your head, what will you do in

the neighboring cell?"[2] The idea is to gain full insight into our mechanicalness and to transcend it. This begins by breaking the simple patterns we are aware of.

These guidelines presented here are just that—guidelines. They aren't prescriptions for behavior or directions for living. They are mainly intended to be food for thought. Some of the ideas presented may be possible for some and very difficult for others. Guidelines can only go so far. In order to make them work optimally, they should arise in a natural, not forced, manner. The ultimate goal is personal freedom and a transcendence of your culture-bound condition.

SEEING DOUBLE

A father said to his double-seeing son: 'Son you see two instead of one.'

'How can that be?' the boy replied. 'If I were, there would seem to be *four* moons up there in place of two.'[3]

This illustrates why it is so difficult to break loose from our consensual, contrived reality. Right or wrong, humans strive for consistency. A selection from Idries Shah's *Tales of the Dervishes* provides an example. First, though, is Shah's commentary.

A recurrent theme among the dervish teachers is that humanity generally cannot distinguish a hidden trend in events which alone would enable it to make full use of life. Those who can see this thread are termed the Wise; while the ordinary man is said to be 'asleep,' or called the Idiot.

This story, quoted in English by Colonel Wilberforce Clark (*Diwan-i-Hafiz*) is a typical one. The contention is constructive: that by absorbing this doctrine through such caricatures, certain human beings can actually 'sensitize' themselves for the perception of the hidden trend.

The present extract is from a dervish collection attributed to Pir-i-do-Sara, 'The Wearer of the Patchwork Robe,' who died in 1790 and is buried at Mazar-i-Sharif in Turkestan.

---

[2]S. J. Lec, *New Unkempt Thoughts;* quoted in Paul Watzlawick, John Weakland, and Richard Fisch, *Change* (New York: W. W. Norton & Co., Inc., 1974), p. 31.
[3]Idries Shah, "Seeing Double," *Caravan of Dreams* (New York: Viking/Penguin, 1968), p. 172.

THE IDIOT, THE WISE MAN AND THE JUG

An idiot may be the name given to the ordinary man who consistently misinterprets what happens to him, what he does, or what is brought about by others. He does this so completely plausibly that—for himself and his peers—large areas of life and thought seem logical and true.

An idiot of this kind was sent one day with a pitcher to a wise man, to collect some wine.

On the way the idiot, through his own heedlessness, smashed the jar against a rock.

When he arrived at the house of the wise man, he presented him with the handle of the pitcher, and said:

'So-and-so sent you this pitcher, but a horrid stone stole it from me.'

Amused and wishing to test his coherence, the wise man asked:

'Since the pitcher is stolen, why do you offer me the handle?'

'I am not such a fool as people say,' the idiot told him, 'and therefore I have brought the handle to prove my story.'[4]

Is there a way out of our logically contrived world—another reality? Certain ancient, Eastern systems of thought claim there is another reality, one that coexists with our ordinary consensus conception of reality, but which is hidden from view. It is "hidden" only in the same sense that perception of color is hidden from those who are colorblind.

ANOTHER DIMENSION

The hidden world has its clouds and rain, but of a different kind.
It's sky and sunshine are of a different kind.
This is made apparent only to the refined ones—those not deceived
by the seeming completeness of the ordinary world.[5]

—Rumi

[4]Idries Shah, "The Idiot, The Wise Man and The Jug," *Tales of the Dervishes* (New York: Dutton, 1970), pp. 61–62.
[5]Idries Shah, *The Way of the Sufi* (New York: Dutton, 1970), p. 104.

In order to be cured of double vision, to get beyond the next cell, to get behind the mirror, we need an eye "operation." There is a saying: "In the country of the blind, the one-eyed man is king." This is true, and then the two-eyed man is a sage.

The "other dimension" or parallel reality is difficult to explain, and is only understood if experienced. We can catch a glimpse of it at times, and to do so, we must first confront our preconceptions and reconsider our frame of reference. In order to catch a glimpse, we first need a new orientation, an alternative cognitive blueprint.

The three stories that follow, chosen from the Mulla Nasrudin corpus of the ancient East, are used (among many others) to help prepare one for an understanding of the "other reality."

THERE IS A DIFFERENT TIME-SCALE

Nasrudin went to a Turkish bath. As he was poorly dressed, the attendants treated him in a casual manner, gave him only a scrap of soap and an old towel.

When he left, Nasrudin gave the two men a gold coin each. He had not complained, and they could not understand it. Could it be, they wondered, that if he had been better treated he would have given them an even larger tip?

The following week the Mulla appeared again. This time, of course, he was looked after like a king. After being massaged, perfumed and treated with the utmost deference, he left the bath, handing each attendant the smallest possible copper coin.

'This,' said Nasrudin, 'is for the last time. The gold coins were for this time.'[6]

MOMENT IN TIME

'What is Fate?' Nasrudin was asked by a scholar.

'An endless succession of intertwined events, each influencing the other.'

'That is hardly a satisfactory answer. I believe in cause and effect.'

'Very well,' said the Mulla, 'look at that.' He pointed to a procession passing in the street.

[6]Idries Shah, "There is a Different Time Scale," *The Pleasantries of the Incredible Mulla Nasrudin* (New York: Dutton, 1972), p. 40.

'That man is being taken to be hanged. Is that because someone gave him a silver piece and enabled him to buy the knife with which he committed the murder; or because someone saw him do it; or because nobody stopped him?'[7]

THE UNSUSPECTED ELEMENT

Two men were quarreling outside Nasrudin's window at dead of night. Nasrudin got up, wrapped his only blanket around himself, and ran out to try to stop the noise.

When he tried to reason with the drunks, one snatched his blanket and both ran away.

'What were they arguing about?' asked his wife when he went in.

'It must have been the blanket. When they got that, the fight broke up.'[8]

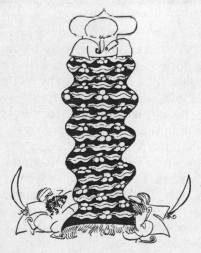

The object of the lessons is that in life, things happen to us and what we think is happening or what we believe it is may be our own contrived/conditioned view—what is actually happening may carry a significance of something that's never been considered before.

[7]Idries Shah, "Moment in Time," *The Exploits of the Incomparable Mulla Nasrudin* (New York: Dutton, 1972), p. 112.
[8]Idries Shah, "The Unsuspected Element," *The Exploits of the Incomparable Mulla Nasrudin* (New York: Dutton, 1972), p. 34.

chapter four
CONTAINER AND CONTENTS

About 1970, Idries Shah wrote *The Book of the Book* (New York: Octagon Press, 1970), a thick, gold-embossed, hardcover book. The book contained an ancient story about a book—a book that warned readers not to mistake the container for the contents. The ancient story contained various stories within the story, with the admonition about not mistaking the container for the contents repeated several times. The entire story took up ten pages; the remainder of the book—more than 150 pages—was blank.

This book by Shah baffled most readers. Naturally, most reviewers went berserk trying to make sense out of it; most experienced alarm, puzzlement, amusement, and frustration. The response was most interesting. Readers and reviewers did not realize the message staring them in the face. The message, of course, is that most people judge things only by appearance, and become indignant when the appearance proves to be fallacious. *The Sunday Telegraph* (March 15, 1970) did succeed in getting the message and printed this comment: "Actually it is—among other things—an extraordinary psychological test, in that it predicts the complete range of possible responses to itself."

What does Shah's book and the response it evoked have to do with this particular book you're now reading? What does it have to do with increasing your mental capacity? To best realize the

Best Sellers

This Week	FICTION	Last Week	Weeks On List
1	**THE RAIN BIRDS,** by Helen von Slite. (Morrow, $11.95.) Gothic romance and adventure on an Australian peat-moss farm.	1	62
2	**STAPLES,** by Judith Glandz. (Viking, $8.95.) A woman's rise in the cutthroat world of Beverly Hills plastic surgery.	2	38
3	**THE CRASH DIET OF '89,** by Paul Bocuse and Paul Erdman. (Pinnacle, $13.95.) Petrodollars and protein supplements.	4	16
4	**GET FLORENCE NIGHTINGALE,** by Irving Clifford. (Harcourt Brace, $10.95.) Nazi plot to abduct the Lady of the Lamp.	3	10
5	**CRAWL SPACE,** by Bev and Biff Goldstein. (Random House, $8.95.) A young, prosperous couple install knotty-pine paneling in the basement of their Connecticut mansion. Death, weight loss ensue.	6	20
6	**TROLLHATTEN,** by R. R. Topiary. (Oxford Press, $16.95.) Miniature world of dragons, fairies and leprechauns underneath a damp log outside Wolverhampton.	5	23
7	**SMILEY'S BIG PROBLEM,** by Jean Le Car. (Knopf, $11.95.) The veteran British spymaster, dead three years, is called out of retirement to find out why House of Lords has defected en masse.	9	6
8	**THE BAMBI DIRECTIVE,** by Robert Luddite. (TAB Books, $5.95.) Deers in Spyland.	7	8
9	**MORE, AND REMINISCENCE,** by Herman Wok. (Little, Brown, $24.95.) Winds of change buffet "typical" American family during Quemoy-Matsu crisis. Fourth in a trilogy.	8	15
10	**FOOLS DIET,** by Mario Putzo. (Lippincott, $8.95.) Life at the top with an overweight hack novelist.		3

This Week	NONFICTION	Last Week	Weeks On List
1	**WHY DID YOU LEAVE BEFORE I FINISHED TALKING?** by Dwayne Wyerd. (Avon, $8.95.) Assertiveness training for stutterers.	1	34
2	**THE COMPLETE SOUTH BRONX MEDICAL DIET,** by Dr. Nathan Perlman, M.D., with Herman Badillo. (Weight Watchers, $10.95.) Eat all you can afford, lose almost everything immediately.	3	16
3	**DWARVES,** by Ulf Larsen, illustrated by Myrlyn Olsen. (Bantam/Peacock, $16.95.) Charming world of the Little People.	4	6
4	**THE LAST CHANCE BEFORE THE EXPRESSWAY DIET,** by Dr. Ronald McPritikin. (Berkley, $8.95.) The famous "fast-food fast," and more.	7	11
5	**SMARMY DEAREST,** by Hermione Frost. (Holt, Rinehart, $7.95.) Growing up unctuous, by the daughter of the famous talk-show host.	2	10
6	**WHAT'S THAT DEAD CAT DOING IN THE CUISINART?** by Thelma Bombast. (McGraw-Hill, $6.95.) The lighter side of household management.	6	17
7	**ALL THINGS SLIGHT AND BEAUTIFUL,** by James Herring. (St. Martin's, $9.95.) Rural doctor treats anorexia in the Yorkshire countryside.	5	16
8	**MEN OF OIL,** by Alistaire Cooke (Exxon, $9.95.9.) Intimate glimpses of the men who made Mr. Cooke possible.		2
9	**HOW TO PROSPER DURING THE COMING VERY WET YEARS,** by Milford Tuff. (Apocalypse, $7.95.) Tax-shelter, boat-building advice.	10	46
10	**THE FUNNY JEWISH DIET,** by Esther Steinmanbergfeld and Marxie Freud Shtetl. (Bintel, $3.95.) Lighthearted spoof of "fad" diets.	8	11

The listings above are based on carbon copies of packing slips from every bookstore in Beverly Hills.

Figure 4–1.

answer, briefly scan the Best Sellers list (Figure 4–1) for the week ending February 25, 1980.[1]

Did you read it? Or did you just scan it? If so, *read* it again, carefully. Most of you (possibly even after a second reading) may not have noticed that it is actually a bogus list—a parody. If that escaped you, the point has been made. The container/content phenomenon reveals our lazy brains. In your daily life, you tend to respond more to form than to content. Becoming aware of this problem will enable you to arouse your sleeping brain.

In a recent article titled "Bafflegab Pays" (*Psychology Today*, May, 1980), Dr. J. Scott Armstrong, currently an associate professor

[1]Andy Meisner's "Best Sellers" from *New West*, (February 25, 1980).

of marketing at Pennsylvania University, reported results of his studies that support the idea, "if you can't convince them, confuse them:"

> 'If you can't convince them, confuse them.' Simply put, this is the advice that J. Scott Armstrong, a marketing professor at the Wharton School, coolly gives his fellow academics these days. It is based on his studies confirming what he calls the Dr. Fox hypothesis: 'An unintelligible communication from a legitimate source in the recipient's area of expertise will increase the recipient's rating of the author's competence.'
>
> Eight years ago, Dr. Myron L. Fox gave a celebrated one-hour talk, followed by a half-hour discussion period, on 'Mathematical Game Theory as Applied to Physician Education.' His audiences were professional groups, including psychologists, psychiatrists, social workers, and educators; afterward, on anonymous questionnaires, they said they found the lecture clear and stimulating.
>
> Fox, in short, was a smashing success. He was also a complete phony—a professional actor whom three researchers had told to make up a lecture of double-talk, patching raw material from a *Scientific American* article into nonsequiturs and contradictory statements interspersed with jokes and meaningless references to unrelated topics.
>
> To test whether such bafflegab also pays in print, Armstrong asked 20 management professors to rank the academic prestige of 10 management journals that had varying degrees of readability according to the well-known Flesch Reading Ease Test. Sure enough, the top-rated journal was the hardest to read; the lowest-rated one, the easiest.
>
> But might not the more prestigious journals have addressed more complex subjects and required more difficult language? Armstrong tested that possibility by rewriting sections from management journals to make them more readable without changing the content—eliminating unnecessary words, substituting easy words for difficult ones, breaking long sentences into shorter ones.
>
> One, for example, originally read: 'This paper concludes that to increase the probability of keeping a (bank) customer in queue, the server should attempt to influence the customer's initial subjective estimate of the mean service to give him the impression that it is small, or attempt to convince the customer that his time value of service is large.'

The rewrite went: "You are more likely to ensure that a (bank) customer waits in a queue if you can get the person to think that he will not have long to wait. Another way to do it is to get the customer to think he will obtain much benefit by waiting."

Armstrong gave easy or difficult versions of four such passages to another group of 32 management professors and asked them to rate, on a scale from 1 to 7, 'the competence of the research that is being reported.' The professors were not told the name of the journal or the author.

Once again, the professors rated the easy version lower than the more difficult one.

Dr. Fox lives.[2]

The point of the study is that people responded to the *context*. Their beliefs about the speaker (or journal article) and the manner in which the presentation was delivered was important; content or subject matter was irrelevant. In fact, the listeners actually were hearing complete nonsense, yet could not even detect it.

We mistake the container for the contents constantly. We buy more expensive cosmetics (even though the actual lotions, creams, and powders are the same as the inexpensive brands) in the fancy wrappings and trappings because we *believe* they are better. If a person calls himself a doctor, wears a white smock, and has an office in a medical building, we assume he is competent, professional, and legitimate. In truth, mediocre, and even dangerous, doctors get by behind a veil of bedside manners, fancy degrees, tasteful offices, prescription pads, and so on. The mistaking of container for contents also explains why we totally believe what the newspapers, television, and radio newsprograms tell us. It probably never occurs to us that the news provided in any given culture is rather biased, selective, and censored (yes, even in the United States). The same news seen on Soviet television and American television is *not* the same. But because something is presented in a certain container (*i.e.*, an acceptable container), we lazily let it sink right into our brains.

Try this simple experiment sometime when you're in the mood to baffle the high school girl behind the counter at your local convenience store. Casually stroll into the place and, with a straight face, ask for "thin cylinders, covered with white paper,

[2]J. Scott Armstrong, "Bafflegab Pays," *Psychology Today* (May 1981).

filled with dried leaves, meant to be set on fire for enjoyment." Or, if that's not enough, ask for "small, rectangular objects, filled with sugar and resin, that are useful for mastication." Odds are twenty to one that the clerk will think that you've just landed from Venus and that she'll send you down the street. The value of this experiment? It illustrates the power of labels, such as "cigarettes" or "gum;" labels, of course, being part of the container.

Ours is an appearance culture—we have trained ourselves to react to appearances, not to think and not to exercise our senses. Our brain muscles need a good workout. We think that the sizzle is more important than the steak. Advertising geniuses know this well. The prices we pay for most items at the market are about 60% for packaging/promotion and probably less than 40% for the product itself. Politicians are also aware of this shortcoming in our nature. Their promotional budgets run in the multimillions (much of which eventually comes out of the taxpayers' pockets) and *what* they say is usually glossed over by form, manner, slogans, appeals to emotion, motherhood, the flag, and so on.

In a recent study, researchers were investigating the nutritional content of the common breakfast cereals. Using rats, they found that in many cases, the rats preferred to eat the cereal *boxes* rather than the cereal. Think about that the next time you reach for a box of Trix on your grocer's shelf...

Allen Funt's television series, *Candid Camera*, also illustrates the container/contents phenomenon. His video captions consist of deliberately contrived, unusual social situations, in which the subject(s) is (are) caught unaware while being filmed by a hidden camera. In these often hilarious scenes, chickens talk, cars split in half, phone booths rise into the air, and drinking glasses dribble. In one sequence, an elevator door opens and out walks a pretty lady, wearing nothing but shoes and a hat. In this scene, repeated with several "victims," very few actually took notice. In another sequence, a woman leaves her car parked in a public parking lot space flanked by two pillars. When she returns later in the day, her car has been rotated 90° (a fork lift truck did the job) straight between the two pillars. Her shock and dismay is evident as she cannot believe her eyes.

Such is the power of the container vs. contents effect. With the nude in the elevator, few people noticed the lady simply because the contents (naked lady) were discordant with the usual container (context). In the parking scene, the woman was shocked for the same reason: the contents (sideways car) did not "fit" with the expected context. The lesson to be learned is that people are so conditioned to context or container, that the reality of an unexpected situation either goes unperceived or is totally disbelieved.

The problem has also infiltrated the human development field, as noted by Robert Ornstein:

> An interested observer of the middle ground is in for some considerable discomfort, since those actively pursuing several interesting ideas have been drawn a bit over the edge. Parapsychology, to the receptive mind, is an area of research which is at least worth some serious, sober, and open-minded scientific investigation. However, one sometimes finds conversations with enthusiasts in the area sliding from a reasonable discussion of a single experiment to the Bermuda Triangle, unidentified flying objects, oddball encounters, or massage techniques. People seeking 'growth' find their needs for personal knowledge blunted and diverted to successful and rich institutions, with massage, sexual athletics, investment schemes, parties, incomprehensible doctrines such as those of Gurdjieff, Kahunism (a flying saucer cult), 'yoga tag,' or simpleminded meditation offered as a substitute for transcendence. Such 'growth centers,' I fear, are to be understood more in the sense of 'growth stocks' and childish self-indulgence than as anything seriously concerned with human development.[2]

It's really remarkable how literally millions of people who refer to themselves as "seekers" believe they are participating in their own growth by wearing guru garb, beads, and turbans; by dancing in circles and by eating berries and nuts. This doesn't mean that real knowledge and real methods for human development don't exist; it's just that their reality (their content) may not necessarily resemble their expected trappings (the container).

One way of getting more from your brain is to be able to distinguish A from B and not to confuse one thing for the other. Added insight into the prevalent container/contents illusion can prove valuable for this exact reason.

[3]Robert Ornstein, *The Mind Field* (New York: Simon & Schuster/Pocket Books, 1978), p. 23.

chapter five
BREAKING MIND SET

———————————

Mark Twain's cat refused to jump on a cold stove because it was once burned on a hot one. Once burned, twice shy, the adage goes. For the most part, we allow our minds to work only in "burn units" when it comes to problem solving. When we come across a new problem, we normally use only our past experience and knowledge in hopes of solving that particular problem. In other words, we rely heavily on what psychologists call *mind sets*— mental blocks or predispositions that can prevent us from achieving a solution even when the answer is obvious or easy.

As an example of mind set, examine Figure 5–1. What your brain "sees" is based on habit and is the *set*.

Like our biceps, the brain needs a bit of flexing now and again to keep in shape. It's as difficult to suddenly have to lift weights with no practice as it is to break mind sets and think creatively under duress with no previous practice.

Before going into specific exercises designed to tantalize your thinking caps, breaking mind sets and going about solving problems can be much easier if you try some of the following steps.

1. Write down the problem. It helps to identify exactly what it is.
2. Redefine or rearrange the problem in as many ways as possible. Each rearrangement or redefinition could point the way to alternative solutions.

THE EYE SEES ...

THE REALITY.

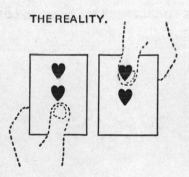

THE BRAIN THINKS ...

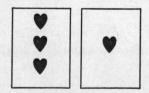

Figure 5–1.[1]

3. Organize the data you have on the problem. Then use a little logic to consider and/or eliminate options.

4. Work backwards. Often the desired goal or solution is more obvious than the actual steps toward it.

[1]Edi Lanners, ed., *Illusions* (New York: Holt, Rinehart and Winston, 1977), p. 30.

31

5. Brainstorm. Often the most inane ideas and suggestions can lead to solutions.
6. Keep track of the problem and watch for any patterns to develop.
7. Consider your assumptions carefully as you think about solutions. Are those assumptions themselves holding you back?
8. Drop it. Sometimes creative inspiration comes when you're not even thinking about the problem.

Following are some exercises designed to help break up those nasty little mind sets. Answers appear at the end of this chapter. Please be sure to attempt each problem before checking the answers.

CIRCLE-SQUARE PROBLEM   Find the area of the square.

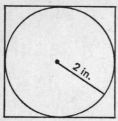

Figure 5–2a. *Circle-Square Problem.*

THE FRUGAL WOMAN   A woman changes her frugal habits and spends money very freely. How many prior circumstances can you suggest to account for this?

HALF OF THIRTEEN   How many different answers can you think of to the question: "What is half of thirteen?"

IT'S IN THE BAG. It was the sixteenth hole in the annual Bob Hope tournament play. The tall, handsome newcomer, who looked very much like Bing Crosby, had an excellent chance of winning. His iron shot had fallen short of the green, and he had a good chance of making a birdie. Smiling broadly and singing 'Thanks for the Memories,' he bounded down the fairway, then stopped short in utter dismay. His ball had rolled into a small paper bag carelessly tossed there by someone in the gallery—although it was whispered that Bob Hope had placed it there. If he removed the ball from the bag, it would cost him a penalty stroke. If he tried to hit the ball and the bag, he would lose control over the shot. For a moment, he stood there pondering over the problem. Then, to Bob's chagrin, he solved it. How did he solve it?

THE SHIPWRECKED SAILOR   What might the hero of the following story do to save his life? Give as many solutions as you can.

A sailor, the lone survivor of a shipwreck, is washed ashore on a remote island inhabited by hostile and primitive natives who capture him. Because he is a stranger and thus threatening to them, the tribe prepares to throw him into a volcano as a sacrifice to their devilgod.

At the last moment, the tribe's sorcerer halts the sacrifice and tells the tribe that this white stranger appears to be their god whose arrival was predicted in religious writings. If he will admit to being that god, the sailor is told, he will be spared and made reigning monarch. The sailor agrees with delight.

After a week of living in splendid luxury, he learns his life is again in jeopardy because the tribe's religious writings also specify that their god can walk on water. Accordingly, a ceremony has been arranged for the next day whereby he will be paddled out many miles into the ocean where, in the presence of the entire tribe, he will perform this miracle.

Breaking mind set is part of the more general activity of problem resolution. Many problems remain unsolved because we keep looking for a solution, rather than a new way of looking at the problem. Sometimes it's good to *reframe* the problem, then the ultimate solution may appear. For example, the New York State Thruway Authority faced the problem of an excessive number of speed-limit violations. They could have, at great expense, hired more troopers to track down the violaters. Instead, they raised the speed limit, and thus eliminated much of the problem, with no increase in the accident rate. In another example, some New York City public schools were having a great deal of trouble keeping students in the classrooms. Many students were wandering through the halls, often running, fighting, and screaming, which was distracting to the students in class. All sorts of remedies were tried, including rewards and punishments, but to no avail. One assistant principal arrived at a solution simply by reframing the problem: She moved the classroom into the halls and called the new plan "the open hall policy."

Another way of facing problems is to consider them as something other than negative; and to refrain from "judging" them. For example, in a recent issue of *New Realities*, Richard Bach (author of *Jonathan Livingston Seagull* and *Illusions*) notes in an interview:

> *Every problem comes to you with a gift in its hands.* Some of us, a long time ago, were troubled with the problem of being trapped in our bodies. We wanted to travel faster than our bodies could run. So we trained animals to carry us, then invented machines to move us. Now we travel faster than sound and we dive into interplanetary space. The little gifts of the problems have been horses and automobiles, radio and airplanes and television. The big gift is the discovery we don't need a body to travel or communicate. A lot of us communicate telepathically, from time to time. The next step is to do it consistently. The step after that is to travel telepathically ... the point is that the idea—problems come with gifts—is a practical tool for discovery.[3]

A similar way of stating the same theme is contained in this old proverb: "A solved problem is as useful to a man's mind as a broken sword on a battlefield." In other words, problems cause one to think, to create, to progress. A person with no problems is no better than a vegetable and can usually be found staring into plain white corners mumbling to himself or herself. Problems—challenges—must be met each day for one to stay sharp.

Another perspective on problems is offered by Frances Vaughan, in her enlightening book, *Awakening Intuition*:

> Frequently when one is faced with a problem or a decision to be made, one is afraid of making the wrong choice. It is sometimes useful to realize that there is usually no right or wrong choice, it is simply a matter of preferring the results of

[2]Richard Bach, *New Realities*, III, no. 3, p. 8.

one choice over another. Rarely is the outcome measurable in terms of right or wrong, good or bad. There is a well-known Zen story that illustrates the point:

A farmer who had just acquired a stallion came to the Zen Master in distress, saying 'Master, the horse is gone, the horse is gone!' for the stallion had run away. The Zen Master replied, 'Who knows if it's good or bad?' The farmer returned to his work feeling sad and miserable. Two days later the stallion returned and brought with him two more mares. The farmer was overjoyed and he went to the Zen Master, saying 'The horse is back and has brought two others with him.' The Master replied, 'Who knows if it's good or bad?' Three days later the farmer was back again, crying because his only son, his only helper on the farm, had been thrown from one of the horses, and his back had been broken. He was now in a body cast and could do no work. The Zen Master again replied, 'Who knows if it's good or bad?' A few days later a group of soldiers came to the farm as they were conscripting all the young men in the area to fight in a war. Since the farmer's son was in a body cast they did not take him.

The story can go on indefinitely. One never really knows if circumstances or choices are good or bad, because one can never really know all the ramifications.[4]

Hence, good/bad mind sets not only prevent us from thinking creatively, but they also prevent us from grasping a wider perspective on life itself.

If you wish to remove the rust that clogs your brain, the "solvent" is to gain insight into your own mental habits and to learn the art of breaking set. In the exercises provided in this chapter, you can begin to appreciate the art, which mainly includes stretching your imagination, entertaining alternatives or options, approaching problems from several angles, and remaining flexible. By viewing problems as challenges rather than as forbidding obstacles, you will be forcing yourself to draw upon your latent creative energies. And for some, this can reawaken their spirit of

[3]Frances Vaughan, *Awakening Intuition* (New York: Doubleday, 1979), p. 168.

experimentation and play, and even reopen their sense of wonder about life itself and its many hidden possibilities.

Exercise Answers

CIRCLE-SQUARE PROBLEM   This problem can cause people trouble because they rely upon habit and will usually begin by computing the area of the circle and fail to notice that by shifting the radius line slightly, it is half the length of a side of the square. The solution of 16 square inches is arrived at by then multiplying 4 × 4.[4]

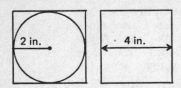

Figure 5–2b. *Circle-Square Problem: area, 16 sq. in.*

THE FRUGAL WOMAN   Some possible answers: She got a terrific raise in pay, she changed jobs for a higher-paying position, she received an inheritance, she won some money, she stole some money, she found a sugar daddy, she married her gynecologist. This exercise forces you to use your imagination. It reveals how it is that less creative problem-solvers tend to be mentally impotent and cling to one or two explanations rather than considering many possibilities.

HALF OF THIRTEEN   Some possible answers: 6.5, a first-grade youngster, six normal human beings and a dwarf, six and a half, almost seven, more than six, not yet a teenager, ⅓, thir/teen, etc.
   This exercise nicely illustrates the advantages of looking at a problem from different vantage points rather than taking the first and only solution that comes to mind.

[4]Paul Chance, "When Rust Clogs Your Brain," *Self* (August 1979), p. 58.

IT'S IN THE BAG   Some possible answers: He could confer with the officials and convince them that this was an exception; that it was acceptable to move the ball from the bag. Or he could cut the bag open with a knife or scissors. Or he could slyly arrange for someone to "accidentally" kick the bag. Or he could take a lengthy break and hope that the wind (providing there is a wind) would knock the bag over.

One of the best solutions is simply to light a match and burn the bag, leaving only the ball and some ashes. Most people don't arrive at this answer simply because their attention is upon trying to remove the ball from the bag, rather than the reverse. Many problems are easily solved by using the "reverse" approach.

THE SHIPWRECKED SAILOR   Some possible answers: He could tell the natives that his water-walking license expired the previous year; that his leg was broken and was in a cast; secretly bury and then "discover" some new religious writings that exclude him from water-walking; that water-walking for gods was not permitted during the spring/summer months; hypnotize the natives into believing he is walking on water; walk on water by standing on a concealed life raft.[5]

---

[5]The last four questions and problems are from Eugene Raudsepp with George P. Hough, Jr., *Creative Growth Games* (New York: The Putnam Publishing Group, 1977), p. 20; p. 40; p. 49.

chapter six
OF TWO MINDS

As you read the words printed on this page, not one but two minds are at work. Do not panic. You are not having a mild attack of schizophrenia. Everyone seems to have these "two minds." These two minds correspond, respectively, to the right and left hemispheres of your brain. As you scan these words, the left hemisphere or "left brain" is working more than the right because this particular side of the brain specializes in verbal, logical, sequential functions, while the right brain is nonverbal, specializing in perception, holistic/simultaneous processing, and intuition (interestingly enough, the left brain controls the right side of the body and the right brain controls the left side).

Why we need two minds instead of one is not well understood at present. Maybe it's like having a spare tire in the trunk. However, Dr. Robert Ornstein of Langley Porter Neuropsychiatric Institute, a well-known proponent of the two-mind theory, suggests the following explanation.

> Perhaps we evolved as we did, with the left hemisphere more involved in sequential information processing than the right, to reduce interference between the two modes. Too much simultaneity in language may produce stuttering or other difficulties; too much sequence in skiing will send the skier

into a tree. We do not have a split brain, but a whole one with specialized parts.[1]

Although contemporary brain researchers continually discover more and more about the bicameral specialization of the brain, due to study of brain injury patients, doctors and scientists have been aware of this curious phenomenon for centuries. Since speech and language are closely linked to thinking, reasoning, and other "higher" mental functions, the left hemisphere has traditionally been referred to as the dominant or *major* hemisphere, with the right considered the subordinate or *minor* hemisphere. "The general view, which prevailed until fairly recently, was that the right half of the brain was less advanced, less evolved than the left half—a mute twin with lower level capabilities, directed and carried along by the verbal left hemisphere."[2]

This prevailing point of view has worked its way into our educational systems, where left-brain logic, reasoning, verbal and analytic skills have reigned supreme; the "three R's" are to this day considered "basics," while nonverbal activities like art and dance are, like physical education, considered diversions, or at best, as good for the body but not for the mind. A child who is good at art but fails at math has learning "problems." The idea is perpetuated by our culture which holds at a premium college degrees, verbal eloquency, the correct spelling of words, and proper grammar.

Although such left-brain skills might be important, unless the skills of the right brain are likewise developed, we are using only half and not all of our brain.

How do we begin to learn to use our right brain (in conjunction with our left brain) thereby maximizing whole brain productivity? Though some may view these pastimes as frivolous, the most obvious solution is to engage in various nonverbal activities, such as sports, dance, music appreciation, art, creative cookery, yoga, crafts, gardening, interior decorating, sewing, and the like

[1]Robert Ornstein, "The Split and the Whole Brain," *Human Nature* (May 1978), p. 78.
[2]Betty Edwards, *Drawing on the Right Side of the Brain* (Los Angeles: J. P. Tarcher, 1979), pp. 27–28.

(poetry, musical composition, and creative writing could be considered cooperative right/left-brain activities). We might refer to these activities as *external* approaches to right brain development since they operate upon the brain from "outside-in."

Another approach could be considered *internal*—mental exercises, activities, or experiences that directly affect the right brain and in turn, by moving "inside-out" can assist in the facilitation of the external skills. Internal approaches to right-brain development are uncommon. However, certain resources are available with some of the more effective systems described in other books and introduced here.

- Edwards, Betty, *Drawing on the Right Side of the Brain: A Course in Enhancing Creativity and Artistic Confidence.* Los Angeles: J.P. Tarcher, 1979.

Dr. Edwards, a professor at California State University, Long Beach, presents a unique course in drawing that applies ideas derived from modern brain research. The reader (or potential Picasso) is drawn into a series of unique experiences that sensitize him or her to the right-brain mode and are designed to release creative potential and drawing abilities. The outstanding feature of Dr. Edwards' course is its capacity to allow nonartists to become highly adept at drawing in only thirty to sixty days.

As an example of Dr. Edwards' methods, consider the following two graphic images in Figure 6–1. A series of exercises are provided to the reader that assist him or her in actually *experiencing* sensations related to the right and left sides of the brain.

L— MODE   *R*— MODE

L-mode is the "right-handed," left-hemisphere mode. The L is four-square, upright, sensible, direct, true, hard-edged, unfanciful, forceful.	R-mode is the "left-handed," right-hemisphere mode. The R is curvy, flexible, more playful in its unexpected twists and turns, more complex, diagonal, fanciful.

Figure 6–1.

Readers are asked to "image" the foursquare, bold L, to see it with the mind's eye and then enlarge the image to form something familiar, like a pyramid or skyscraper. Then the curvy R is to be imaged and transposed to curved objects, designs, motion, and so on.

In another exercise, the reader is asked to draw the following picture (Figure 6–2), which is upside down.

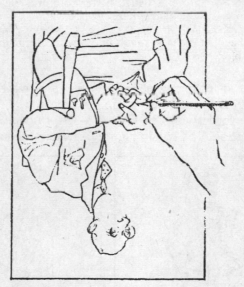

Figure 6–2.

Dr. Edwards refers to this as *inverted drawing*, which forces a distinct, cognitive shift from the dominant left-hemisphere mode to the subdominant right-hemisphere mode:

> Once you've started drawing, you'll find yourself becoming very interested in how the lines go together. By the time you are well into the drawing, your L-mode will have turned off (this is not the kind of task the left hemisphere readily takes to: it's too slow and it's too hard to recognize anything), and your R-mode will have turned on ...
>
> This puzzle puts the logical left brain into a logical box: how to account for this sudden ability to draw well, when it (the

know-it-all left hemisphere) has been eased out of the task. The left brain, which admires a job well done, must now consider the possibility that the disdained right brain is *good at drawing*.

More seriously speaking, a plausible explanation of the illogi-cal result is that the left brain refused the task of processing the upside-down image. Presumably, the left hemisphere, con-fused and blocked by the unfamiliar image and unable to name or symbolize as usual, turned off, and the job passed over to the right hemisphere. Perfect! *The right brain is the hemisphere appropriate for the task of drawing.* Because it is specialized for the task, the right brain finds drawing easy and enjoyable.[3]

As proof of her ideas, Dr. Edwards provides the following samples of art from her beginning students.

The two drawings in Figure 6–3 were copied from a right-side-up portrait. The two in Figure 6–4, from the inverted portrait.

Figure 6–3.

Psychologist Jerome Bruner, referring to Dr. Edwards' course, has commented: "This is a marvelously fresh approach to drawing and will make people not only draw better, but *see* better."

• Savary, Louis M. and Margaret Ehlen-Miller, *Mindways: A Guide for Exploring Your Mind.* New York: Harper & Row, 1979.

This is an intriguing book that provides a complete series of ideas and exercises about many aspects of the mind, creativity, and

[3]Ibid., p. 53; p. 55.

Figure 6–4.

life. The book presents a "whole-mind" approach that emphasizes both left- and right-brain functions and the interplay of each. Evocative photographs and quotations are strategically placed throughout the book to enhance its effect. Chapter headings include: *The Evolving Mind, The Masculine-Feminine Mind, The Sharing Mind, Whole Mind/Whole Body, Gateways to Creativity, Beyond Whole-Mind Learning.*

"The Closet and Your Mind" is an example of an exercise for your right/left mind:

> A trip to your clothes closet can provide you with a simple and effective illustration of how the two hemispheres of your mind work. When you take out a piece of clothing, you can probably tell where you got it, what size it is, the proper time and place to wear it, and how much it is worth on the market. All of this reasoning you do with your left brain. But now begin with your right-brain feeling-sense to describe how the clothing makes you feel when you wear it. Does it make you feel warm, happy, relaxed, all dressed up, uncomfortable? Experience responding both ways to pieces of clothing until you get to where you can actually feel the change from left- to right-hemisphere activity.[4]

- Gallwey, Timothy, *The Inner Game of Tennis.* New York: Random House, 1974 and Gallwey, Timothy, and Bob Kriegal, *Inner Skiing.* New York: Random House, 1977.

[4]Louis M. Savary and Margaret Ehlen-Miller, *Mindways: A Guide for Exploring Your Mind* (New York: Harper & Row, Pub., 1979), p. 5.

These two books on *inner sports* describe a unique approach that emphasizes the mental aspects of what are customarily considered physical endeavors. Although no reference is made by these books to the left and right brains, another writer, Thomas Blakeslee in *The Right Brain* has discovered the parallel. The objective of the inner-game approach is to provide exercises which help turn off inner chatter (left brain) while performing a nonverbal, right-brain activity. (Ever notice that when you think about exactly how you're going to serve the ball, you can't do it?) Gallwey refers to the verbal mode as Self 1 and nonverbal mode as Self 2. Blakeslee notes:

> Though Gallwey makes no mention of the physical location of Self 1 and Self 2, it is clear that they are actually the left and right hemispheres of the brain. While either hemisphere is capable of controlling both sides of the body, only the right hemisphere is capable of instantly reacting to the many simultaneous spatial variables of a tennis game. The split-brain experiments showed us that the hemisphere that feels most strongly that it can handle a problem will tend to take control. By emphasizing nonverbal knowledge of tennis skills, the right brain is given a clear, competitive advantage.

> The opposite of the inner-game approach is to fill the student with verbal descriptions of theoretically proper movements. The student's left brain thus 'thinks it knows a lot' and tends to interfere with natural movements.

> One of the techniques Gallwey uses to disengage the verbal self during practice is distraction: While the ball is hit back and forth, the student is asked to say 'Bounce!' whenever the ball bounces and 'Hit!' whenever it hits a racket. This verbal task keeps the verbal consciousness occupied and ensures that body and racket movements stay under right-brain control.[5]

- Raudsepp, Eugene, with George P. Hough, Jr., *Creative Growth Games*. New York: Harcourt, Brace, Jovanovich, 1977.

Raudsepp is president of Princeton Creative Research, Inc., an organization devoted to the advancement of creative problem solving and decision making in industry, business, and education. *Creative Growth Games* presents seventy-five stimulating problems designed to "expand your creative powers and everyday problem-

[5]Thomas Blakeslee, *The Right Brain* (New York: Doubleday/Anchor, 1970), p. 79.

solving activities." These games or problems are not the usual brain-teasers you find in the backs of magazines at the dentist's office that only tax the logical, rational left brain. Instead of being simple one-answer problems, these exercises force you out of your logical mind set and increase perception and imaginative potential. For example, try this simple problem: In exactly five minutes, list all possible uses for a wooden block or blocks (any size).[6]

Some possible answers can be found at the end of this chapter.

Following upon the success of his first book, Raudsepp has recently come out with another brain-buster, *More Creative Growth Games*. New York: Perigee/Putnam, 1980.

- Ornstein, Robert E., *Common Knowledge*. New York: Viking/Compass, 1975.

This is a collection of strange and odd news stories, many of which describe real-live events or happenings that run contrary to expectation and logic. The effect of these stories is to "strengthen patterns of vision, which enable us to see the improbable, the unusual, the 'paranormal' as they occur before our eyes. They shake us out of our fixed, arrogant assumptions about what can happen in life."[7] According to Ornstein, these stories are closer to the truth of living than the stylized, stereotyped reportage we commonly associate with "news." An example is given in Figure 6–5.

- Train, John, *True Remarkable Occurances*. New York: Potter, 1978.

This is another book which has compiled actual cases from history as well as news articles about the unusual. An example is seen in Figure 6–6.

- Siegel, Jules, and Bernard Garfinkel, *The Journal of the Absurd*. New York: Workman Pub., 1980.

This is the latest book about strange and "improbable" news items. The collection is very broad, and like the other two books listed above, can assist one in helping to break stereotyped

[6]Eugene Raudsepp with George P. Hough, Jr., *Creative Growth Games* (New York: The Putnam Publishing Group, 1977), p. v; p. 14; pp. 103–4.
[7]Robert Ornstein, *Common Knowledge* (New York: Viking/Compass, 1975).

THE FISH THAT KILLED A SEAGULL

Brixham, England

Members of a yacht club say they saw a fish kill a seagull.

They said when the bird dived Wednesday to grab a fish in Brixham Harbor, the fish grabbed the seagull, pulled it beneath the water and drowned it.

United Press

Figure 6–5.

thought patterns, as well as releasing momentary dosages of insight and illumination.

The two sides of the brain and the balancing of both halves is surely a valuable and important endeavor; however, it helps to consider that there is undoubtedly more to the whole-brain approach than just this. The bicameral division of the brain hemispheres is what might be termed a horizontal approach: right-left.

Another way of dividing the brain is up-down or vertical, and in this view there are *three* brains. At the lowest level there is the brain stem, which has an arousal function (without it we would be comatose and no fun at parties); at the next level up, there is the limbic system, which specializes in needs, drives, and emotion (feeding, fight, flight, and sex), and the top level, which is the cerebral cortex. The horizontal, left-right hemispheres are located at this upper level.

In addition, at the base of the brain, and, seemingly attached to the brain, is the cerebellum. This is a sort of "fourth brain" that

46

Mars and Venus

"During the fray [May 12, between part of Grant's army and a Confederate detachment], a [soldier] staggered and fell to earth; at the same time a piercing cry was heard in the house near by. Examination of the wounded soldier showed that a bullet had passed through the scrotum and carried away the left testicle. The same bullet had apparently penetrated the left side of the abdomen of ... [a] young lady midway between the umbilicus and the anterior spinous process of the ileum, and become lost in the abdomen. This daughter suffered an attack of peritonitis, but recovered.... Two hundred and seventy-eight days after the reception of the minié ball, she was delivered of a fine boy, weighting eight pounds, to the surprise of herself and the mortification of her parents and friends.... The doctor ... concluded that ... the same ball that had carried away the testicle of his young friend ... had penetrated the ovary of the young lady, and, with some spermatazoa upon it, had impregnated her. With this conviction he approached the young man and told him the circumstances. The soldier appeared skeptical at first, but consented to visit the young mother; a friendship ensued which soon ripened into a happy marriage."*

*The American Weekly, November 4, 1874; quoted in Gould and Pyle, Anomalies and Curiosities of Medicine. Philadelphia: The Julien Press, 1896.[8]

Figure 6–6.

has developed in parallel fashion with the cerebrum; it is a complete brain in miniature, which also has its own right and left halves. Although traditionally considered by scientists to have a relatively minor function—that of aiding motor coordination—modern research is finding additional functions for the cerebellum, such as its shared role with the limbic system in monitoring emotion and the sensations of pleasure/displeasure. Although knowledge about the cerebellum is scarce, one standard physiology textbook states: "In many ways, the cerebellum is just as

[8]John Train, *True Remarkable Occurrences* (New York: Potter, 1978), p. 36.

complex as the cerebrum."[9] While the cerebellum is only 11% of the total weight of the cerebrum, because of its extensive folds and fissures, it is *two-thirds* the size of the cerebrum, in respect of surface area.

Drawing upon various lines of research, Stan Gooch, in his book, *The Paranormal*, makes a case for the unsuspected significance of the cerebellum, especially its role in subconscious functioning, dream experience, and, possibly, extrasensory perception. He explains quite clearly how the cerebellum evolved parallel to the cerebrum and notes that,

> ... the cerebellum and its consciousness do not only work at night in our dreams. I believe they are also at work in all the various trance conditions—in mediumship, in hypnosis, under the influence of drugs, in love, in women especially and in children especially.

> Women have larger cerebella than men. Women dream more than men. Women are more superstitious then men. Children have more active cerebella than adults. Children are more superstitious than adults ...

> Yet a further dimension comes into play here, that of human evolution. Asiatic and Eastern peoples have larger cerebella than Westerners. (Do they dream more than Westerners? We do not know. I believe it will be proved they do) ... We (modern man) are a hybrid creature, a cross between the Neanderthal and Cro-Magnon varieties of early man. Neanderthal man had an active religious life ... and we believe that Cro-Magnon took over many of Neanderthal's religious practices—though I believe he in no way had the same control over actual paranormal phenomena. *Neanderthal had a larger cerebellum than Cro-Magnon.*[10]

Speculative as they may be, Gooch's ideas are original and are extrapolated from scientific data.

In considering the entire brain and in attempting to entertain possibilities beyond those offered us by left/right brain research, we might also note certain comments by the author and Sufi authority, Idries Shah. In one of his latest books, *A Perfumed Scorpion*, he alludes to contemporary left/right brain studies in light of ancient, esoteric sources of understanding.

[9]C. T. Morgan and E. Stellar, *Physiological Psychology* (New York: McGraw-Hill, 1950); quoted in Stan Gooch, *The Paranormal* (New York: Harper & Row, Pub. 1978), p. 200.
[10]Stan Gooch, *The Paranormal* (New York: Harper & Row, Pub., 1978), pp. 206-7.

An Eastern position on left-and-right hand brain function might well be that, however useful it can be to define them, there is yet another mode of cognition—though it may be connected with the interplay of the two."

Shah is implying something more than the now recognized functions of the right and left sides of the brain. This other "mode of cognition" would probably be best understood by a Sufi who undergoes the experience, however Shah intimates the process on the next page:

> And it is worth remembering that this perception by the Sufi is regarded by him as linked with a cosmic intuition, which drives him to work in the field of human education of the Sufic kind. In this feeling, he agrees with Einstein that, 'The cosmic religious experience is the strongest and noblest driving force behind scientific research.'[12]

To conclude, when people say "I'm of two minds about that," they may correctly be describing an actual physiological process in their heads. And most of us tend to use one side more than the other. In order to get maximal output from our brain, a balance between right and left sides should be the aim. Beyond that there are other higher capacities that may emerge once both sides are functioning in greater concert.

Exercise Answers

POSSIBLE USES FOR A WOODEN BLOCK OR BLOCKS   If you listed just a few uses for blocks, you might be considered average—but it is average to be unimaginative; this is because most cultures and educational institutions train us to consider only the familiar and the obvious. Besides the familiar uses, wooden blocks can be used in many other ways: as a paperweight, a weapon, bookends, firewood, to build a raft, to break windows, as a doorstop, as a hammer, as an ashtray when hollowed, as a candle holder, to make wooden shoes, as a footrest, for weight lifting (infants), as a bug killer, to sell for a living, etc., etc.

[11]Idries Shah, *A Perfumed Scorpion* (London: Octagon Press, 1979), p. 18.
[12]Ibid., p. 19.

chapter seven
LOGIC BOX

Ever since the days ancient Greeks sat around resting on their laurels and Aristotle discovered thinking, logic has enjoyed a certain celebrity status and reverence for its "correctness." After all, we always say smugly, "It's the *logical* thing to do." This implies a certain aura of sanity, doesn't it? However, this mode of thought is worshipped far beyond its true value; it is not the only, nor the right way, to think. There are serious restrictions and limits to the use of logic that should be recognized.

Logic is a Tool

Very simply, logic is a tool of thought and, like all tools, it's limited to specific uses. After all, you don't use a hammer in order to sweep the sidewalk. While it may apply in certain situations, in some situations, other tools of thought are more applicable. For example, in problem-solving situations, lateral thinking (see Chapter 8) is often more effective. For creativity, visual thinking is usually better. And beyond that, intuition can be superior to all the rest.

Secondly, when this "tool" of logic is being used "correctly," it may be used in a trivial manner or even may be irrelevant to the

50

situation. So, a shovel may be used to build giant sand castles, but sand castles can't be lived in—unless you happen to be a sand crab. And when someone who doesn't bear the faintest resemblance to a sand crab is building a sand castle that he actually believes he can live in ... well, the result is ludicrous.

Paranoia and Logic

One of the most common forms of logic entails the deduction of conclusions from certain premises. But if these initial premises or assumptions are false (they often seem to be)—deductions are useless.

All of which brings us to the timely subject of paranoia ("Stay calm, act cool, nothin's gonna happen OHMYGODTHERE'SA-COPFOLLOWINGME, oh no officer, not me, I wasn't speeding ISWEARTOGODHE'SGETTINGREADYTOPULLMEOVER, relax, relax..."). Paranoia is distinguished by its airtight logic. Some very "intelligent" people function as paranoiacs, because in paranoia, everything seems logical—it can all be justified.

For example, the paranoiac believes there is a plot against him. Once he accepts this basic premise, everything he says makes complete sense—especially to him. Once he assumes this plot (although he won't recognize it as a mere assumption), everything that happens to him is interpreted through this "logical" framework: he sees sinister, coded threats while reading the comics section of the Sunday newspaper; "Have a nice day" is interpreted to mean he will be assaulted when he rounds the corner; the woman smiling seductively at him over the cabbages in the supermarket is a modern-day Mata Hari, and so on.

You see, logic and paranoia do go hand-in-hand. That doesn't mean that the use of logic is always a form of paranoid functioning; it does, however, point out the interrelationship that may often occur. This can be quite a serious problem when the process operates between nations, such as it now does between Russia and the United States—a great example of global paranoia. What makes it so easy to be sustained is that the logic underlying the pathology between the countries is so airtight.

Logical Paradox

The limitations of logic are seen quite clearly in so-called "logical paradox"—also known as logical deadends. Because logic is a rule in the correct use of statements, many statements can be devised that can't be resolved by logic. An example comes from Epimenides of Crete who once uttered this bit of brilliance:

"All Cretans are liars."

The logical problem is this: if he is correct (telling the truth), then he, too, is lying. And conversely, if he is lying, then he can't be telling the truth. This is a logical inconsistency that *cannot be resolved by logic*. This sort of example clearly exposes the impotence of logical reasoning.

One way out of the problem is to bypass logical or theoretical reasoning and to take a more empirical approach. Okay, so possibly some Cretans are liars (notably Epimenides), but others are not. Perhaps, to take things one step further, Epimenides was a liar who occasionally uttered an honest line or two.

"A voice in the night cried out: 'There's no such thing as a voice in the night.'"

Again, a logical contradiction, but not a problem if the logic is disregarded. The conclusion is that something is happening (a voice is crying out) and that the particular string of words being used is useless. In other words, truth is beyond the use of words and logic.

All logical paradoxes aren't the same, and all are not resolved in the same manner. But their solution is never arrived at through the use of logic—that is the point to understand. They yield logic helpless and their solution lies at another frame of reference (outside the confining box of logic).

In a certain village, there is a man (so it goes) who is a barber. The barber shaves all and only those men in the village who do not shave themselves. Query: Does this barber shave himself?

A hair-splitting thought, indeed!
The problem is obvious: Any man in this village is shaved by

the barber if and only if he is not shaved by himself. Therefore, the barber shaves himself if and only if he does not. We are in trouble if we say the barber shaves himself and we are in trouble if we say he does not. Ah, that double-edged blade ...

Since logicians are so obsessed with the power of logic, most will rarely admit its limits and weaknesses (that would be like a P.O.W. *admitting* he's been brainwashed). So, in mulling over this foamy dilemma about the barber in the village, one well-known logician—W.V. Quine in an article entitled "Paradox" that appeared in *Scientific American*[1]—solved this case (in all earnestness) by smugly asserting this solution: "No such village can exist!" Oh, what brilliance. Thus the logicians remain consistent (logical) by arriving at an absurd conclusion and then attaching an acceptable term: *reductio ad absurdum*. Presumably, this legitimizes his conclusion.

A similar logical paradox was "solved" in 1904 by the philosopher Bertrand Russell, while the rest of the world was trying to figure out what to make of this new century, he became stifled by a particular paradox and even obsessed with arriving at a logical resolution. In attempting to solve logical paradoxes, similar to the one by Epimenides of Crete, Russell admitted:

> ... the two summers of 1903 and 1904 remain in my mind as a period of complete intellectual deadlock. It was clear to me that I could not get on without solving the contradictions ... but it seemed quite likely that the whole of the rest of my life might be consumed in looking at that blank sheet of paper. What made it the more annoying was that the contradictions were trivial, and that my time was spent in considering matters that seemed unworthy of serious attentions.[2]

In conjunction with Alfred North Whitehead, Russell eventually "solved" this paradox, which was then published in *Principia Mathematica* in 1913. They called their solution "The Theory of Logical Types;" but, it is only a "solution" by fiat or definition (not unlike Quine's *reductio ad absurdum*). To quote Russell and White-

---

[1]W. V. Quine, "Paradox," *Scientific American* (April 1962), pp. 84–96.
[2]Bertrand Russell, *The Autobiography of Bertrand Russell*, vol. I (London: G. Allen and Unwin, 1967), p. 51; also quoted in Patrick Hughes and George Brecht, *Vicious Circles and Infinity* (New York: Viking/Penguin, 1975), p. 13.

head: "Whatever involves *all* of a collection must not be one of that collection."[3]

So, in reference to the "All Cretans are liars" statement, Russell and Whitehead believe that the statement is not to be considered a part of what he (Epimenides) is talking about. The statement and its object (class referred to) must be kept separate.

And so, a particular statement by a Cretan about all of the statements made by Cretans is not itself to be considered part of what he is talking about. (Say *that* ten times real fast.)

But, on the other hand, who says this has to be so? What Russell and Whitehead are claiming is that we are not to take Epimenides' statement seriously—which is exactly what Russell was trying to accomplish in 1903–1904: not to take a triviality seriously. It seems, then, that Russell's solution in and of itself is a logical paradox. He was irked with himself for taking something admittedly trivial as serious, and was able to resolve *his* problem by establishing another trivial law or theory that in and of itself was trivial and whose aim it was to claim: "consider trivial statements as trivial." This is similar to making up your own rules to benefit you as you play a vigorous game of Monopoly.

One last example:

Drawing Hands by M.C. Escher, shows a strange loop. A hand is drawing a hand, which in turn is drawn by that hand. Such apparent paradoxes can be resolved only by taking into account a higher level system—the unseen artist who is drawing both hands.[4]

So, if paradoxes or problems are going to be solved, it is often useful to leave one frame of reference and move to another. If you can't see out a window because it's cracked, either replace it or look out another one. It wouldn't hurt if logicians could do the same relative to their own frame of reference—their Chinese puzzle box: get out of the box. Or, let's put logic aside and realize that truth can lie outside the maze of words and logic.

[3]Ibid., p. 13.
[4]Paraphrased from Howard Gardner, "Strange Loops of the Mind," *Psychology Today*, vol 13, no. 10 (March 1980), p 78. Figure 7–1. on page 55 is a print of an Escher lithograph (VAGA Beeldrecht, Amsterdam/VAGA, NY, 1981). Collection of Haags Germeentemuseum.

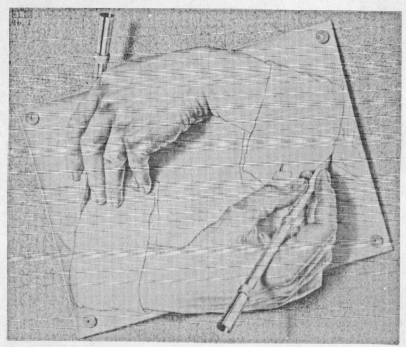

Figure 7–1. *Drawing Hands*

Using Illogic

Another limitation of logic is that often something totally *illogical* can have value or be truthful. This includes much of what happens to people in daily life—after all, how could a flat tire or a run in a brand-new pair of pantyhose be *logical*? Often, illogical occurrences pop up in news articles (see Figure 7–2. on page 56).

Another example is Paradoxical Therapy. In a recent book, *Making Things Better by Making Them Worse*, Dr. Allen Fay advocates all sorts of paradoxical or contrary-to-logic therapeutic strategies, many of which work surprisingly to cure the patient of the problem. For example, thumbsuckers are broken of the habit by being advised to suck their thumbs all of the time. Similarly, incessant smokers have overcome the cigarette habit by being told to smoke *more*. This paradoxical therapy was even used to get more

55

Giant snowball kills youth

LONDON (UPI) — A 7-year-old boy was crushed to death by a giant runaway snowball as he was playing near his home in Telford, police said on Wednesday.

Anthony Bowers died Tuesday night when the snowball, five feet in diameter and weighing several hundred pounds, buried him alive.

Police said he had been building a snowman on a hillside with two companions, when the huge ball suddenly began rolling away. Anthony chased after it, slipped, and was crushed by the giant ball.

Figure 7–2.

motorists to use seatbelts, after it became clear that government public service announcements ("Buckle up to save your life") were simply not working. To get people to use them, Dr. Fay advised people not to use them. "I would tell them crashes help keep hospital beds occupied ... it is important that orthopedic surgeons, plastic surgeons, oral surgeons, and others in the medical establishment have patients..." This is the old, "I'll give you something to *really* cry about" theory.[5]

Related to the illogical approach is the "Power of Contrary Thinking," or the ability to forfeit the forward moving stream of "logical" thinking and to think in opposites, in contraries.

Look at some simple commercial successes around you and you will see good examples of the Power of Contrary Thinking in action:

For many years, producers of infant strollers seemed to be in a competition which paralleled the one going on at the time in the automobile industry: how to put more chrome, vinyl upholstery, ornate designs and pizzazz into their products. I remember thinking one day as I shopped for a British-made baby carriage, "Does my child really need to have a vehicle

[5]Allen Fay, "Paradoxical Therapy Solves Problems By Making Them Worse," UPI, *Arizona Republic* (June 1978).

56

that resembles the Coronation Coach in which Queen Elizabeth rides on important occasions?" Several bright young businessmen must have noted this trend toward absurdity and, through Contrary Thinking, reasoned that the market was getting too far away from basic consumer need. They invented and marketed the Umbrella Stroller—a simple, portable, folding infant stroller—and made a fortune in the process. Good business acumen requires looking at the market in both directions: where it is heading, and also (in the Contrary Thinking direction) what part of the market is being vacated.

The BIC Company has grown by leaps and bounds through recognizing that, contrary to the belief that the status value of a product is important, consumers hate to have to go to the trouble of getting things repaired. BIC has successfully marketed simple ball point pens, cigarette lighters and shavers that have one great advantage: when they stop working, you throw them away and buy another one. While other companies specialized in the top end of the field—the expensive, gold-plated lighters or pens—BIC saw and seized the opportunity to dominate the throwaway market—another triumph of Contrary Thinking.[6]

Logical Extension

Nasrudin arrived at an all-comers' horse-race mounted on the slowest of oxen. Everyone laughed: an ox cannot run.

'But I have seen it, when it was only a calf, running faster than a horse,' said Nasrudin; 'so why should it not run faster, now that it is larger?'[7]

The most blatant error in the correct use of logic is what is known as the fallacy of "more of the same"—or, when the solution becomes the problem. This derives from the logical extension of a basic principle in problem solving: if something is going wrong, apply the corrective, its opposite. If it rains, use an umbrella or seek shelter; if it's cold, put on warm clothing or add heat. Very

[6]Sidney Lecker, *The Money Personality* (New York: Simon & Schuster, 1979), pp. 87–88.
[7]Idries Shah, "The Child is Father to the Man," *The Exploits of the Incomparable Mulla Nasrudin* (New York: Dutton, 1972), p. 80.

logical. But consider some other examples. If drinking is a social problem, then provide restrictions. Well enough. If that doesn't do, add more restrictions, as was done during the Prohibition era. But what happened? More drinking and alcoholism than before. Pornography was once considered a problem in Denmark, and greater legal restrictions were adapted. But in spite of these restrictions and massive censorship, pornographic activities actually increased. (The problem finally was resolved by an unlogical approach: pornography was legalized and liberalized to the point everyone began to ignore it and it lost most of its attraction.)

In a chapter titled "The Potato Chip Imperative" from Dr. William James Haga's humorous but insightful book *Haga's Law*, (New York: William Morrow, 1980), Haga described another variant of the logical extension problem, "The Linear Escalation Fallacy." This is the idea, usually associated with bureaucracies, of, "if a little bit does a little good, a whole lot is bound to do wonders." It's well known that some arranging and standardizing can help keep things in order, to reduce uncertainty and chaos. True to logic, bureaucracies and "organizations" carry the step much further:

> With only seven days to prepare, Israeli commandos easily rescued hostages at Entebbe Airport. A similar raid by American forces to nab 55 POW's out of Son Tay prison camps near Hanoi took fourteen months of preparation and 170 rehearsals. When the commando team finally got there, the Son Tay camp was empty.[8]

And further:

- The U.S. Postal System is in the process of eliminating its already complex five-digit zip code in favor of a nine-digit system.
- Citizens of New York City are governed by 1,487 different governments, boards, and agencies.
- In California, a loaf of bread carries with it an accumulation of 454 different taxes.
- Pesticides, widely introduced to control disease and improve crops, are now poisoning the food of farm animals and our drinking water.
- The Oklahoma House of Representatives recently used several of their sessions to debate a proposal which would require a man

[8]Paraphrased from Dr. William James Haga and Nicholas Acocella, *Haga's Law* (New York: William Morrow and Co., 1980), p. 43.

to obtain a woman's written consent—in duplicate—before they engage in sexual intercourse. According to Representative Cleta Reatherage, who introduced the bill, the purpose of the consent form was "to inform her that she might become pregnant, and that childbirth could result in serious health problems."

And the logical trend continues: more skyscrapers (and less pretty landscapes), more jails (and crime rates increasing), more weaponry, bigger bombs, more nuclear reactors (with greater threat potential to citizens), more and more taxpayers' money being used to fight drug abuse (with more and more people using drugs, including prescription drugs), more cars (and more traffic jams), and so on. This Game Without End, or "the more you eat, the more you want" mentality will continue as long as we persist in our love of logic.

Theoretical Instances

Theories have a great attraction to us, simply because they are so logical, and theories do abound. Everyone has their own pet theory about something or other, and the sciences are abundant with them. Psychology, for example, has hundreds of theories. But often, the theory makes more sense than the reality, and errors abound. If you are a Freudian, a dream about snakes and dark caves will always have sexual connotations. If you're a Jungian, then the same dream will simply be a reflection of your collective unconscious. In Primal Therapy, you are made to scream (since *all* neurosis is the result of repressed emotion), while in Rational Therapy you change your thinking ("*all* neurosis is due to faulty thinking").

Because of the logical correctness and intellectual appeal of their theories, it is rare that the theorist is exposed. But when this does happen (*i.e.*, when reality is encountered), the results are predictable, if not amusing.

THEORETICIAN

Once upon a time there was a man of great repute for his wisdom, who lived in a certain town.

He told the people about life and death, about the planets and the earth, about history and about every kind of unknown thing.

One day a dam burst and the people went running to him to tell them how they could solve the problem.

The wise man drew himself up to his full height.

'I think that you should avoid asking such puerile questions from a man of the mind. I am not a water engineer, I am a theoretician.'[9]

Many books on mental development and "how to improve your thinking" contain chapters on deductive logic—how to think logically/clearly. They will usually provide you with a list of the "rules of logic" and you are expected to learn them. The center-piece of the whole logical system is Aristotle's famous categorical syllogism. The standard example is this:

All men are mortal.
Socrates is a man.
Therefore, Socrates is mortal.

Once you learn this, you are then presumed better able to "think straight." Usually you will be asked to then solve some reasoning tests to check your logic. Here are a couple of sample tests:

All poisonous things are bitter. Arsenic is not bitter. Therefore, arsenic is not poisonous.

All true Americans have a marked sense of humor. This sense of humor is noticably lacking in all Communists. So, no true American can be a Communist.[10]

Both tests prove to be logical; but the problem is obvious—they have no application to reality.

And this is why the rules of deductive logic aren't contained in this book. Granted, it may be useful to apply logic in some situations, but ever since Aristotle, we have been overtrained in this game of yes and no and a balance needs to be reached. Besides

[9]Idries Shah, "Theoretician," *The Magic Monastery* (London: Jonathon Cape, 1972), p. 59.
[10]Rudulf Flesch, *The Art of Clear Thinking* (New York: Harper & Row, Pub./ Barnes & Noble, 1951), pp. 59–65.

logic, we can now appreciate the illogical and the paradoxical, and can begin to free our intellect in order to see things in a new way.

In a wider scope, our entire lives may seem logical to us because of the cleverness of our valued intellect, but even it can deceptively put us on the wrong track without our ever realizing it.

THE SHORT CUT

Walking home one wonderful morning, Nasrudin thought that it would be a good idea to take a short cut through the woods. 'Why,' he asked himself, 'should I plod along a dusty road when I could be communing with Nature, listening to the birds and looking at the flowers? This is indeed a day of days; a day for fortunate pursuits!'

So saying, he launched himself into the greenery. He had not gone very far, however, when he fell into a pit, where he lay reflecting.

'It is not such a fortunate day, after all,' he meditated; 'in fact it is just as well that I took this short cut. If things like this can happen in a beautiful setting like this, what might not have befallen me on that nasty highway?'[11]

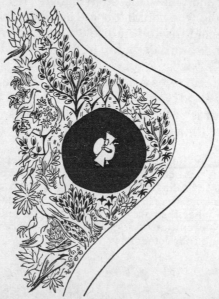

[11] Idries Shah, "The Short Cut," *The Exploits of the Incomparable Mulla Nasrudin* (New York: Dutton, 1972), p. 148.

chapter eight
THINK AGAIN

We all know Idea people. People who, while driving along, while taking a shower, while doing the laundry, will come up with brilliant, clever and/or new ideas. Then there are the other, equally intelligent people who couldn't come up with a new idea even if an all-expense-paid trip to Paradise was at stake. Why is this so? Apparently, Dr. Edward de Bono, in the forward to his book, *The Use of Lateral Thinking*, wonders the same thing. "Why do some people always seem to be having new ideas while others of equal intelligence never do?"[1]

The answer isn't the excessive abuse of Vitamin E; rather it's the use of lateral thinking.

> This method of thought is different from the traditional logical method: it is more concerned with the generation of new ideas rather than the refinement of old ones; with possibility than with certainty; with richness than with rightness; with the use of chance rather than its rejection. Lateral thinking doesn't replace the traditional, logical thought-process—vertical thinking—it's complementary.[2]

[1]Edward de Bono, *The Use of Lateral Thinking* (London: Jonathan Cape, 1967), p. 5.
[2]Edward de Bono, *Lateral Thinking* (New York: Harper & Row, Pub./Colophon, 1973).

Just because a person recently filled out an application to become a Mensa member, it doesn't necessarily mean that he or she has the ability to think laterally/creatively—or to think at all, for that matter. In fact, a person with a high I.Q. is usually better at vertical, logical thinking. That's not to say that only dense people are artists while only geniuses are systems analysts—exceptions abound.

Lateral thinking is not something that your genes are zapped with during creation, but rather a skill that can be learned by anyone. In his several books, Dr. de Bono provides various techniques which, when put into practice, can assist in the development of lateral thought.

What's the difference between vertical and lateral thinking? With vertical-logical thinking, one begins with certain assumptions, premises, and concepts, and generates ideas/deductions in a sequential, step-by-step procedure to arrive at the answer. With lateral thinking, however, one questions the original assumption-premises-concepts one *begins* with. ("What do you mean, chocolate is fattening?"). In other words, vertical thinking accepts the first stage as given, while lateral thinking is first-stage thinking. It questions your initial concepts; your initial perceptions or way of looking at the situation in question. As mentioned before, vertical thinking is used to answer a question or to find a solution to a problem. On the other hand (or mind), lateral thinking asks whether the question or problem is appropriate. Sometimes, even the way a question or problem is framed is a problem in itself. Lateral thinking can be used as a device in reframing the question/ problem itself, thereby assisting in the solution of the problem.

In summary, vertical thinking begins at the second stage. Arrogance often accompanies vertical thinking because it assumes the correctness of the concept at the first stage. It restricts the possible ways you may look at a problem by rejecting alternatives at the start. So, the next time you want to call someone arrogant, you may want to call them "vertical" instead. Obscure, but effective.

Lateral thinking, on the other hand, begins at the first stage. It helps you by adding flexibility (you can strain your brain without it). It gets you to question your assumptions and to examine your initial concepts ("Maybe chocolate is good for the libido...?").

With vertical thinking, then, you refine and elaborate upon established concepts; with lateral thinking, you change concepts and ideas.

For example, in the early days of horseless carriages, arm signals were devised to let drivers behind them know which way you were going to turn. As carriages became modernized and referred to as "cars," automatic arms were invented that flipped out when the driver pulled a lever. Cars had these gadgets for some time until one bright thinker reframed the problem; instead of considering these gadgets as arms, he changed the concept to "direction" and electrical turn signals (flashers) were invented.

Because of our magnificent obsession with traditional, established thinking, we are fascinated with logic, math, computers, and pocket calculators. But these things only carry out linear, mathematical processes. They cannot think creatively (although some computers do seem creative enough to effectively screw up our lives with a given number of mistakes). They are *programmed* in that they are fed "first-order thinking" information and then process it sequentially. Though some computer fiends may protest, computers can't be inventive, can't change ideas, can't generate new ideas and, are poor at creative problem solving. Computers merely process givens.

With the advent of lateral thinking, the emphasis has now shifted to the following:

• What questions we ask the computer.
• What ideas we feed the computer.
• What use we make of the computer's output.

Thinking, although it's a natural process, tends to scare many people. If all jobs required frequent thinking, most people would not work. Many people do not know how to think, even though they may seem like intelligent folk. The myth about thinking is that it is some special, academic process that's only practiced by men with grey beards and flowing robes; that it's some sort of semantic game played by philosophers according to certain rules that originated in the mind of Aristotle and were refined by successive philosophers since.

But that is really formal, logical, vertical thinking. Boring when used alone. Thinking may be conceived as a practical, active, and enjoyable process—in any case, it's something we can use every day.

Let's consider some techniques of lateral thinking adapted from de Bono. Since vertical thinking works with familiar, established concepts and ideas, it is a form of patterned thinking. Right versus wrong. Lateral thinking is most useful in disrupting established patterns of thought.

Techniques: A Quick Course in Lateral Thinking

The first technique is called *generating alternatives*. With vertical thinking, we often believe there are only one or two alternatives to a problem or situation. By generating alternatives, we loosen up those rigid beliefs. One way to get the mind moving in this direction is to do like the traffic officers supposedly do: set a quota and fill it. In other words, find as many alternatives to a problem or situation as you can—even after you've found the "right" answer.

Try this exercise: Half of a picture is obscured. What you can see is a man balancing on the edge of a ledge along the side of some building. What's he doing? Try to come up with as many possibilities as you can. For this particular exercise, let's set a quota of four alternatives: He's a stunt man. He's about to commit suicide. His girlfriend's husband just came home. He's fleeing from a burning building. And so on. Ever notice how generating one alternative often leads to another?

Challenging assumptions is another refreshing approach to breaking out of old thinking ruts. Most of our lives are based on assumptions (wheels are round for ease of movement, reading is a good way to learn, most food should be cooked before it is eaten, and so on); facts of life that we never challenge because, well, just because it's so. But says who?

Try this little exercise: A landscape gardener is given instructions to plant four trees so that each one is exactly the same distance from each of the others. Okay. Usually, most would try to arrange four dots on a piece of paper so that each dot is equidistant from the other dot. Impossible. Not really. Most assume the trees must be planted on level ground. But if one tree is planted on the top of a hill and the other three are planted at the sides of the hill, this makes them all equidistant from one another (in fact, they are at the angles of a tetrahedron). This exercise is not to prove that you must challenge everything in life—someone might get riled at your challenges and get an urge to slap you—but an occasional "why?" throughout the day will keep you from being imprisoned by cliches and assumptions.

With vertical thinking, you must be "right" at each step before you can progress in your thinking; if not, you must repeat that thought-step over and over until it's "right." In other words, you're constantly judging things, and this stifles creativity.

Suspended judgement is a technique you can use in lateral thinking that aids in breeding new ideas. Don't do without judgement completely, just hold off a bit; don't say "no" right away—let yourself go down a few blind alleys. You never know what you'll find at the end of them. As a classic example, Marconi succeeded in transmitting wireless waves across the Atlantic ocean through following up the erroneous idea that waves would follow the curvature of the earth. (Luckily, the electrically charged layer in the outer atmosphere, the ionosphere, bounced the wireless waves back to earth.)

Design projects are also a good way to stimulate lateral thinking. Maybe you're not an engineer or an architect, but put all that aside. Refrain from thinking "this will never work" and grab a piece of paper, a pencil, and some imagination. Boldly set forth and design: an apple-picking machine, a cup that can't spill, and a device to help cars park. Redesign: the human body, a new type of clothes, and a chair. Organize: a way to build a house very quickly, a method to shop easily, and a new method to travel quickly but inexpensively. This is not practice in design; it's practice in lateral thinking. No medals or awards will be handed out. You're just learning to think *differently*.

In looking at any given situation or in attempting to solve a problem, we rely upon certain concepts or dominant ideas as if they were life preservers on a sinking ship. Sometimes these key concepts are useful, but often they act as a barrier, preventing solutions (a person will never learn to swim while clinging to a life preserver). For example, if we believe we must fight drug abuse in our society, then we become engaged in a battle. But battles rarely solve things. *Concept changing* is the deliberate exercise of detecting key concepts or dominant ideas in a given situation and temporarily suspending them in order to allow consideration of other, less obvious concepts. A specific approach is "dropping a concept" in which we agree (with ourselves or others) to conduct our thinking/dialogue on the problem or situation without mention of the key concept. Thus, in considering drug abuse, "fight" or "battle" are dropped, and we continue on. New concepts tend to materialize—we might consider medical approaches, revise our attitudes about drugs, question our social structure (since most drug abuse is with prescribed drugs), and so on.

People who spend all day working behind desks very frequently take up leisure activities like running or hang gliding to break themselves of their established workday patterns. The same can be said of thinking. Often the best way to get away from established patterns of thinking is to use the *reversal-method*; i.e., turning something around, thinking completely opposite of an established pattern to generate new ideas or to solve a problem. Try turning these subjects around: going on a holiday, teachers instructing students, and salespeople helping customers. Interesting what it can lead to ... a holiday going on you, students teaching instructors, customers helping salespeople. In each of these randomly chosen examples, by further use of your imagination, you can arrive at some interesting ideas. Spend your holiday by throwing a gala party at your home. By getting students to teach, they may need to learn their subject matter more thoroughly than normal. By getting customers to help salespeople, they may experience gratification and make it more likely they will buy something.

A good method to use in the development of lateral thinking is *brainstorming*. In this kind of group interaction, all judgement is suspended—it's okay to say or suggest practically anything, no matter how ludicrous. Brainstorming's greatest contribution to the development of lateral thinking is cross-stimulation, in which an idea from one mind stimulates something else from another mind. One idea leads to or develops another. Write down what you come up with, follow it up, then evaluate.

Using *analogies* is another good way to get going on a problem or idea. By comparing one thing or situation to another, you tend to look at things differently. For example, eating French fries is eating French fries. But, using analogy, eating French fries can be likened to—or generalized to—nutrition, the act of consuming, the acceptance of a specialized kind of food by the American masses, recreation, acceptance into society, and so on. The main usefulness of analogies is as vehicles for functions, relationships, and processes, which can be transferred to the problem or situation under consideration to help restructure it.

A distinguishing feature of the mind is its ability to choose, to attend to something deemed important. In considering any situation or problem you usually attend to some specific elements of the situation. If your bathtub overflows, you first try to shut off the water. *Entry point* refers to the part of the problem or situation you *first* attend to. But if the situation is complicated or confusing, or if you are having trouble solving the problem, you may need to switch over to a new entry point. As an example, a man was changing his flat tire, when all four bolts rolled into a storm drain. He was incapable of figuring out what to do, and became quite upset, trying to decide what to do next. He was about to call for help, when a young boy watching him, suggested a simple solution: take one bolt from each of the three other wheels and use them on the spare replacement until the man can drive to an auto parts store. Whereas the man's attention was on the spare tire and the lost bolts, the boy's focus was on the three other tires.

Random stimulation is a technique that's effective in problem solving or in generating new ideas. With vertical thinking, you usually only deal with what is relevant and don't waste your time considering other sources of information that have nothing to do with the problem or situation. However, random stimulation is provocation; it disturbs established patterns. To get some random stimulation try the *exposure method*. For example, physically, go somewhere you've never been. Accept all random input. Don't close yourself off from other people's ideas. Expose yourself to different fields. If you are a computer programmer, find out about fashion design. The stimulation could be useful to your present job. You could get random stimulation a bit more formally. Use a dictionary to pick out a random word. Study it, use it. Go to a library and pick out a random book or magazine. Apply it. With random stimulation, you can connect and apply information to almost any situation or problem you have.

A Device For Successful Thinking

Vertical thinking relies on two basic devices—yes and no, otherwise known as the *yes-no system*. Our society is based mainly upon this system. Something new comes up, and, based on our established concepts/ideas/patterns, our minds evaluate it and we accept ("yes") it or reject ("no") it.

In the other half of the brain, so to speak, lateral thinking goes beyond this yes-no system. It is more concerned with perceptions and with changing and creating ideas. To help suspend our trusty yes-no reflexes, de Bono has devised a new concept—Po. Not since man first said "maybe" in the cave days has something like this come along. Yet, Po is not really new; it is new only because de Bono has identified this device and has given it a name. Traditionally, Po has been used by inventors, poets, artists, and so on, but the device is available to everyone.

What is Po? It's the temporary suspension of yes-no. It's the bypassing of premature judgements. It opens up the way to alternative considerations.

Something not possible in vertical/logical, sequential thinking is known as the *intermediate impossible* when you're using Po. The intermediate impossible is an idea or suggestion (normally applied in solving a problem or in creating a new product, invention, and so on) that does not fit. It is seemingly impossible, but it can lead you out of a rut toward something new. For example, considering ways to improve the automobile. A Po response might be "Cars should have square wheels."

This gets you temporarily away from the notion that cars must have round wheels—this fixates you upon wheels. The fact

that Po cars should have square wheels may lead you to alternatives to the wheel, since the objective is left to *transportation*, not to
wheels. This may lead to the idea used in hydrofoil boats—in
which jets of air are released downward allowing the car to propel
forward without wheels.

Lateral thinking is a practical device to use for yourself and
your own problems, but why stop there? We've been relying so
heavily on vertical thinking for so many eons, but society still has
many problems. Over and over again, we fight crime by punishing
criminals, we try to cure addicts by making them give up drugs,
we try to fight poverty with more money. But that's using vertical
thinking; we can't move from step A to step B unless everything is
"right" first.

Perhaps if lateral thinking was applied to wider horizons,
recurring problems such as crime, addiction, and poverty may be
solved ... or maybe there wouldn't be problems any more.

chapter nine
BEYOND THE LINEAR BRAIN

An ant one day strayed across a piece of paper and saw a pen writing in fine, black strokes.

'How wonderful this is,' said the ant. 'This remarkable thing with a life of its own, makes squiggles on this beautiful surface, to such an extent and with such energy that it is equal to the efforts of all the ants in the world. And the squiggles which it makes! These resemble ants: not one, but millions, all run together.'

He repeated his ideas to another ant, who was equally interested. He praised the powers of observation and reflection of the first ant.

But another ant said: 'Profiting, it must be admitted, by your efforts, I have observed this strange object. But I have determined that it is not the master of this work. You failed to notice that this pen is attached to certain other objects, which surround it and drive it on its way. These should be considered as the moving factor, and given credit.' Thus were fingers discovered by the ants.

But another ant, after a long time, climbed over the fingers and realized that they comprised a hand, which he thoroughly explored, after the manner of the ants, by scrambling all over it.

He returned to his fellows: 'Ants,' he cried, 'I have news of

importance for you. Those smaller objects are a part of a large
one. It is this which gives motion to them.

But then it was discovered that the hand was attached to an
arm, and the arm to a body, and that there were two hands,
and that there were feet which did no writing.

The investigations continue. Of the mechanics of the writing,
the ants have a fair idea. Of the meaning and intention of the
writing, and how it is ultimately controlled, they will not find
out by their customary method of investigation. Because they
are 'literate.'

Following is Idries Shah's commentary on the ants and the
pen:

This allegory, based upon an argument of Rumi's (*Mathnavi,
IV*) was used by the teacher Saad el-Din Jabravi, the founder of
the Saadi Sufi School.

The intention in this version is to admit the usefulness of the
scientific ('ant') method of investigation, while insisting that
another kind of knowledge ('literacy') not normally associated
with man, must be acquired in order to make sense of life.

Jabravi died in Damascus in 1335. His tales are still current,
accompanied by the argument that allegory is essential to the
human mind to envisage ideas which cannot be captured by
any other method.[1]

Our approach to life is often like that of the ants. We perceive
small bits and pieces and then make grandiose generalizations. We
can call this approach linear, logical, or piecemeal. But there is
another mode of perception—intuitive and holistic perception—
that grasps the relations between the parts directly, rather than by
sequence or deduction.

To illustrate how easily most of us fall into the "piecemeal"
kind of thinking, consider the two sets of circles in Figure 9–1. In
each case, count up the number of solid circles as quickly as
possible.

[1]Idries Shah, "The Ants and the Pen," *Caravan of Dreams* (New York: Viking/
Penquin, 1972), pp. 180–81.

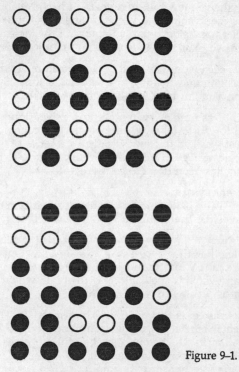

Figure 9-1.

The usual way to handle this problem is to count the solid circles in each case. This is a sequential, step-by-step operation. But when you come to the second set of circles, it would have been quicker and easier to look at the *total* set, notice the open circles and subtract these from the total number of circles arrived at by multiplying the number of circles along one edge of the rectangle times the number along the other edge. The manner in which the latter problem is solved is mainly nonsequential: It is arrived at by observing the whole set simultaneously and deriving a more efficient result.[2]

Tony Buzan, in his book *Use Both Sides of Your Brain*, adds the following observation on the linear mind trap:

[2]Edward de Bono, *Lateral Thinking* (New York: Harper & Row, Pub./Colophon, 1973), p. 184.

For the last few hundred years, it has probably been thought that man's mind worked in a linear or list-like manner. This belief was held primarily because of the increasing reliance on our two main methods of communication: speech and print.

In speech we are restricted, by the nature of time and space, to speaking and hearing one word at a time. Speech was thus seen as a linear or line-like process between two people.

Print was seen as even more linear. Not only was the individual forced to take in units of print in consecutive order, but print was laid out on the page in a series of lines or rows ... the advantage of this way of thinking is so long-standing that little has been done to contradict it.

Recent evidence shows the brain to be far more multidimensional and pattern-making, suggesting that in the speech/print segments, there must be fundamental flaws.

It is easy to point out that when words travel from one person to another, they necessarily do so in a line, but this is not really the point. More to the point is, the question: 'How does the brain which is speaking, and the brain which is receiving the words, deal with them internally?'

The answer is that the brain is most certainly *not* dealing with them in single lists and lines. You can verify this by thinking of the way in which your own thought processes work while you are speaking to someone else. You will observe that although a single line of words is coming out, a continuing and enormously complex process of sorting and selecting is taking place in your mind through the conversation.

Similarly, the listener is not simply observing a long list of words like someone sucking up spaghetti. He is receiving each word in the context of words that surround it.

The agrument for print is also weak ... the mind is perfectly capable of taking in information which is non-linear. In its day-to-day life, it does this nearly all the time, observing all those things which surround it, which include common non-linear forms of print: photographs, illustrations, diagrams, etc. It is only our society's enormous reliance on linear information which has obscured the issue.[3]

One of Buzan's major contributions to nonlinear thinking is

[3]Tony Buzan, *Use Both Sides of Your Brain* (New York: Dutton, 1976), pp. 84-87.

his method of *pattern notes*, which is a technique for organizing thoughts and material. Instead of listing one's key ideas/information about a given topic in linear, list-like fashion as is typical with this approach, you begin with the central concept and *design* a holistic pattern of ideas that connectively branch out. Buzan lists the advantages of this method over the linear approach:

1. The center or main idea is more clearly defined.
2. The relative importance of each idea is clearly indicated. More important ideas will be nearer the center and less important ideas will be near the edge.
3. The links between the key concepts will be immediately recognizable because of their proximity and connection.
4. As a result of the above, recall and review will be both more effective and more rapid.
5. The nature of the structure allows for the easy addition of new information without messy scratching out or squeezing in, and so on.
6. Each pattern made will look and be different from each other pattern. This will aid in recall.
7. In the more creative areas of note making, such as essay preparations, and so on, the open-ended nature of the pattern will enable the brain to make new connections far more readily.[4]

As an example of the success of this method, see Figure 9–2. on page 76. Here are the "best notes" in linear writing of a fourteen-year-old boy, and his pattern-notes on English.[5]

Most books and practically all nonfiction are arranged in sequential fashion. One chapter leads to another and a break in the sequence would seem to obscure understanding. We have become accustomed to this linear approach and learn to expect it. But this "linear set" can also prevent us from getting the most from our brain. The other approach, simultaneous thinking/knowing, lets us get much more from our brain (at the very least, allowing us to gain new insights and possible alternatives), and operates by allowing us to group the overall relationships between parts, rather than by way of a sequence of tidy deductions.

[4]Ibid., p. 89.
[5]Ibid., p. 73.

7) SETTING   Time + places in which the novel is situated

8) IMAGERY   the kind of images the author uses to describe (usually by simile or metaphor)

9) SYMBOLISM   one thing stands for another
The witches in Macbeth signifying evil

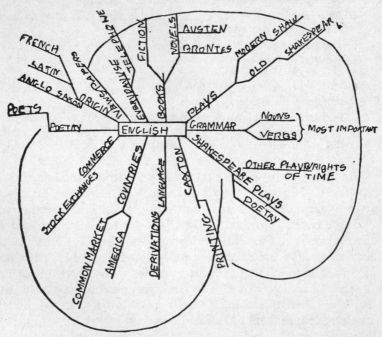

Figure 9–2.

Let us examine the writings of a nonlinear thinker, Joël de Rosnay and his book, *The Macroscope: A New World Scientific System.* From the Introduction:

The general organization of *The Macroscope* is in the image of the approach that it advocates and describes: my medium is also my message.

This approach does not lend itself readily to conventional forms of communication. It has been necessary to 'invent' even the organization of the book; to 'invent' the means of communication that it intends to establish.

I have, therefore, turned my back on the classic organization of the 'linear' book, in which ideas, developments, and chapters follow one another in sequential form. That is a corridorlike, tunnel-like book, a one-way traffic in which one understands the end only when he has assimilated the facts given at the start.

I prefer the 'intersecting' book to the linear book. You pick it up where you want; you pursue it according to your desires by following several simple and precise rules from the beginning. Thus, if you wish, you will be able to compose a book á la carte, one that corresponds as much as possible to your own interests and to what you hope to find in it. That is why the chapters and sections of *The Macroscope* are relatively independent modules, all of which play a part in leading toward the vision of the whole.[6]

de Rosnay then goes on to examine such subjects as 'The Systemic Revolution: A New Culture,' 'Energy and Survival,' 'Information and Interactive Society,' 'Time and Evolution,' and 'Values and Education' through his macroscope, a symbolic instrument made of a number of methods and techniques borrowed from very different disciplines.

Masters of the unlinear and the nonsequentially designed book are the Sufis. They have been aware of the value of nonlinear, holistic thinking/knowing centuries before the current findings and interest. In describing his own (as well as traditional) writings, Idries Shah notes:

It will not have escaped your notice that I have been moving from one illustration to another without necessarily linking the two; that we have alternated arguments and verbal statements

[6]Jöel de Rosnay, *The Macroscope: A New World Scientific System* (New York: Harper & Row, Pub. 1979), p. xv.

with tales and imagery; that stress has been placed upon allegory and imagery within a sequential narrative which is not, however, expressed in historical, personality or logical terms for very long. I have chosen this method of approaching this subject in order to attempt the switching of attention, which is characteristic of the Sufi literary techniques of stimulus and what is technically termed 'scatter', to give you a glimpse in twentieth-century terms, of the atmosphere and method of the classical books of the Sufis of the past.

... The selection in this case is made to offer a kaleidoscope of impulses, some of them familiar, some of them intended to encourage interest, others to stimulate disagreement. But a major intention behind such materials is to enable the reader or hearer to observe his own reactions, as well as merely to react or to memorize.

It is amusing to record that this technique, so easy to observe when one is on the lookout for it, has so confused and so often annoyed scholarly, 'sequential' no doubt, analysts, that they have had very hard things to say about it.[7]

The Sufis employ this nonlinear or *scatter method* of writing for several reasons. The switching of attention is one, used for the purpose of preventing the mind from slipping into its lazy, accustomed patterns. This upsetting of expectations also serves to shock the mind into momentary hyperconsciousness.

Being a Sufi is to put away what is in your head—that which is imagined truth, preconception, conditioning—and to face what may happen to you. For the typical Western mentality, this isn't exactly easy. We tend to fill our minds with excess baggage constantly.

Dr. Edward de Bono, in his several books about lateral thinking, has provided numerous valuable insights into the limitations of the sequential approach. One predominant limitation he refers to is the *sequence trap*.

SIMPLE MODEL WITH PLASTIC PIECES

Figure 9–3 shows what happens when some plastic pieces are given in a certain sequence to a person who is asked to arrange them so as to give the simplest possible shape. The first two

[7]Idries Shah, *A Perfumed Scorpion* (London: Octagon Press, 1979), p. 42.

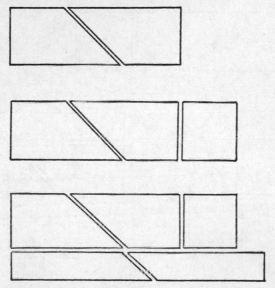

Figure 9–3.

pieces are immediately arranged to form a rectangle. The next piece to arrive is simply added to the existing triangle to give a longer rectangle, as shown. But the next two pieces cause a lot of trouble, because it seems impossible to arrange all the pieces to give a simple shape.

ESCAPE FROM THE SEQUENCE TRAP

The sequence in which the plastic pieces have arrived has determined the way they are arranged. You build on existing arrangements and go on building on these in a continuous fashion. But with the plastic pieces it is possible to make progress only by going back and re-examining the long rectangle (Figure 9–4). Though this was a very good arrangement at the time, you find that another arrangement is possible—a square. Once you have restructured the arrangement to give a square, the next stage is absurdly easy. I have used this model on over two hundred occasions in the course of my lectures and no one has ever reached the square. The sequence trap is much more powerful than we realize.[8]

[8]Edward de Bono, *Po: A Device for Successful Thinking* (New York: Simon & Schuster, 1972), pp. 76–77.

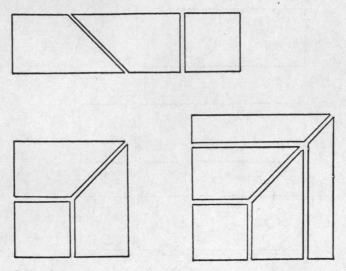

Figure 9–4.

This revealing exercise is fun on paper, but takes on an even broader meaning when you transpose those plastic pieces to life itself. As de Bono notes, the sequence in which things happen in life has everything to do with the ideas and attitudes we hold. A person who was rich before the Depression, then lost his fortune during it, would face life quite differently than a person who made money during the Depression. A narrow attitude toward Blacks in America is based predominantly on the historical sequence of slavery in this country. Women's strong desire to assert themselves via careers and education is due almost exclusively to their historical role definition and then the force of the women's movement in the late sixties and early seventies. Thus, it's easy to see that the outcome of all familiar human experience depends mainly on sequence. How often have you said to yourself, "If only..."

Thus, the concept of lateral thinking (de Bono's major contribution on mind expansion) relies heavily upon nonlinear, nonsequential techniques. A distinguishing feature of lateral thinking is that it provides us with methods that allow us to deliberately and willfully introduce discontinuity into our ongoing thought process (a horrifying thought within the hallowed hallways of our civilization's law schools).

On the other hand, vertical, logical thinking seeks to establish continuity: one thing must directly follow another. However, with lateral thinking, you can make deliberate jumps. There are no rules that determine your flow of thought. Lateral thinking utilizes a multiplicity of methods that do not require sequential justification. It's the end or creative results that will justify the means.

World-renown chef and author, Paula Wolfert, is a prime example of a lateral thinker (and doer). When she teaches a cooking class, she runs amuk in the kitchen, thinking out loud, seemingly throwing things together at the last minute without rhyme or reason. However, when you see her dinner presented— and then taste it—you'd think she had diagrammed every last bit of parsley into a highly organized cooking plan.

The message of this chapter should now be clear: conventional brain functioning has habitually accustomed itself to a linear, step-by-step mode of operation. In order to achieve a more comprehensive level of consciousness, it would pay to attune yourself to nonsequential experience. Because of the comparative unfamiliarity of this approach, the sources quoted in this chapter (Buzan, de Rosnay, Shah, de Bono) may be consulted to give you a proper start.

chapter ten
THE BIG PICTURE

Being nearsighted has its advantages. Without the aid of glasses, one doesn't see the tiny flaws, the bumps, or the cracks in the facade. The imagination fills in the blanks. Being "nearsighted" mentally also has its advantages. One sees only what one wants to see.

However, with the advantages, the disadvantages come right along; like a coin, there are two sides. *Perceptual myopia* and *partial mentation* can be likened to a need for contact lenses for the mind; these failures in our thought processes restrict our possibilities.

Perceptual myopia can be otherwise described as selective perception—you see only what you want to see or what you have been taught to see. Partial mentation is thinking only "part way"—recognizing one possibility (out of many); seeing only one side instead of all; or thinking that a part is a whole.

On the other end of the mental spectrum, there's holistic (or wholistic) thinking, which is a relativistic concept since we rarely know when we have the total picture. However, this concept of holistic thinking is a positive alternative when contrasted against a more limited, constricted, specialized, and overanalytical approach.

Holism is quite the trend lately—everything from holistic dentistry to holistic pet-raising—particularly in the field of thought, where rational analysis has dominated for so long. But *holistic* has become a catch-all label for all sorts of things, and like *guru* has lost its essential meaning.

> Flirtations, the population crisis, genetic counseling, inflation, job problems, heart attacks—they are part of our lives and, if we are to have a complete vision of human nature, we need to deal with them all.
>
> Properly speaking, this endeavor should be called holistic, which means 'seeing things whole.' But the word 'holistic' has become the property of the flaky side of the human sciences and no longer belongs to those who are interested in completeness. In medicine, the word has become the rallying cry for the wild, unsupported fringes of healing. In education, it has become a byword for the simple refusal to teach reading and writing. In spirituality, holistic religion has become the fountain of instant self-improvement courses and screaming therapies—tantrum yoga.
>
> Whatever these things are, they are not holistic—they simply replace one idea with another. This degeneration is sad, for although 'holistic' is the correct word to describe a complete look at human nature, it is now unusable because of the meaning it has been given by its partisans. The same thing has happened to the word 'gestalt,' dragged down by the therapy of that name. It is time to put all these labels to sleep, perhaps for three years. Their naps might clear our heads.[1]

Instead of putting these labels to sleep, however, we might still find them useful, provided the admonition is heeded.

Following are some of the stumbling blocks that prevent us from seeing the big picture; from attaining more holistic thinking.

Interpretation and Bias

Interpretation and bias are interrelated processes. They are those mental processes that emphasize one view or one side to the exclusion of all others. Most commonly, this is an unconscious, subtle phenomenon whereby the person undergoing the process

[1]Robert Ornstein, "A Letter from the Director," *Human Nature* (January 1979).

is unaware that his or her view is only one of several possibilities, thus failing to see the validity of other possibilities. Take, for example, a press conference. Two educated, experienced reporters from two different newspapers attend the same conference. Assuming both are fairly honest and have several scoops of integrity, they will do their best to present the facts of the conference accurately. And nine times out of ten, the two stories will come out sounding quite different, almost as if the two reporters had attended two different press conferences.

The tendency to interpret one way or to be biased is the symptom of a lazy brain—and we are all guilty of it. And just as we need to continually fight general laziness in our daily lives, we need to continually be alerted to the laziness of the brain. Look at these illustrations in Figure 10–1 that reveal just how the brain tends to go down the path of least resistance.

In the first drawing, what did you see? A rabbit or a duck? In the second sketch, did you see a young lady or an old woman?

Since laziness and inertia are characteristic of human nature, bias and the interpretational flaws can be found most everywhere. Even in science, where objectivity is the goal, interpretation and bias are ever-present. In a book titled *Rival Hypotheses: Alternative Interpretations of Data Based Conclusions*, authors Schuyler W. Huck and Howard M. Sandler present one hundred problems consisting of brief summaries of actual research studies and the conclusions derived from the data. In each case, there was a contained direct or indirect claim that the original writer (usually unknowingly) wanted readers (as well as himself) to believe. In all these studies, an alternative claim can be found and sometimes even more. An example is provided here. Before reading Huck and Sandler's solution, try to determine the alternative interpretation(s).

DIRTY WORDS

One of our favorite stories is that of the psychologist who asked his client to respond to line drawings of a square, a circle, and a triangle. The client interpreted the square as a window in a house and gave a lurid account of what was going on inside. This was followed by equally lurid descriptions of the activities viewed through a porthole (the circle) and a keyhole (the triangle). When the client was told by the psychologist of his sexual hang-ups, he replied, 'Sexual hang-

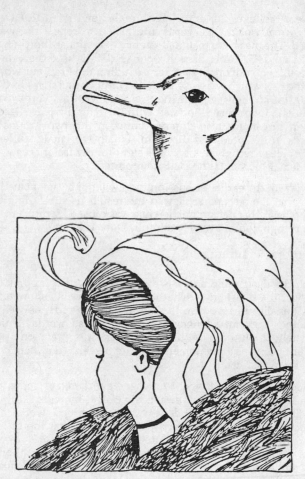

Figure 10–1.

ups! You're the one with all the dirty pictures.' This story reminded one of our students of the following study.

Perceptual defense is a term used in psychology to refer to our perceptual system's ability to fend off unpleasant stimuli. It is a way of sticking our heads in the sand without getting our hair dirty. One researcher used seven socially taboo words ('whore,' 'bitch') embedded within a list of eleven neutral words ('apple,' 'dance') in order to establish the phenomenon of perceptual defense as one involving the optical system.

Sixteen college students (eight male, eight female) were shown each of the 18 words and asked to repeat the word aloud. The measures included latency of response (how long it took), and Galvanic Skin Response (GSR, used here as a measure of emotionality). After excluding the first four words on the list, which were used as a warm-up, differences in GSR were found between the neutral and critical words with greater emotionality associated with the critical words. Recognition thresholds also differed between the two groups of words in the predicted direction. Finally, the male students were able to recognize the words significantly faster than were the female students (no statistic reported).

In view of the earlier discussion, you will not be astonished to find that the researcher viewed the results as supporting the hypothesis that perceptual defense was caused by problems in the recognition of aversive stimuli. Do you agree?

Authors' Solution:

Both the design and analysis of this study are appropriate to answer the question of whether college students show more emotionality in response to socially taboo words, as well as whether they take longer to identify those words. Unfortunately, in our opinion, the researcher's interpretation of the latter finding as a phenomenon of the perceptual system does not seem justified.

Since it would take longer to recognize unfamiliar words, the researcher did consider the plausible rival hypothesis of unfamiliarity of college students with the critical words and rejected it, no doubt correctly, on the basis that the college students he knew were quite familiar with such words. However, he failed to consider the possibility that, although the students stated when asked that they responded equally promptly to all words, the delays for the critical words were a result of a slight (or possibly strong) reluctance to blurt out these words in a laboratory setting. As the study was conducted considerably before the women's liberation movement began, we feel safe in suggesting that the temper of the times could be used to support the rival explanation. We suspect that these results would not appear if the study were conducted today.[2]

[2]Schuyler W. Huck and Howard M. Sandler, *Rival Hypotheses: Alternative Interpretations of Data Based Conclusions* (New York: Harper & Row, Pub., 1979), p. 91; p. 195.

The solution is quite plausible and offers another alternative to that claimed by the researcher. But alternatives to the authors' solutions are also possible. Did you think of any? One important factor could be the sex of the experimenter. If the experimenter were female, possibly the opposite result would occur, with males showing a greater delayed response. Another interpretation might be that emotions interfered with making a vocal response and that this was more marked in females because of a difference in physiology. Also, if the experimenter was the same researcher who authored the study, possibly his or her expectations as to the predicted outcome of the study may have subtly influenced the subjects' response in the desired direction.

Naturally, other solutions are possible, but the object of the exercise is to gain insight into the multiplicity of interpretations possible in a situation and not to accept the one-and-only obvious view. Reading the book by Huck and Sandler and attempting to solve the one hundred exercises (before reading the authors' solutions) is excellent practice in sensitizing you to the interpretation-bias effect in everyday life and can add some flexibility to your brain.

Although the interpretation-bias effect can make half-wits and numbskulls out of all of us in everyday experiences, it is more serious when manifested at national and international levels. For most Americans—particularly those who were born in the prebaby boom generation—the Vietnam War was necessary to stop the spread of communism, and it was even considered justified to break the 1954 Geneva Conference agreement to do so. The Communists (*i.e.*, the Soviets), naturally, had a mirror-image interpretation: The United States was waging war in an area of the world where there was no immediate threat to its own security. It was doing so to spread capitalism, and thus, broke the Geneva agreement. At the time of this writing, the exact mirror-image interpretation effect is taking place in response to the Soviet's activity in Afghanistan. The Americans see this as the Soviet takeover of an innocent, defenseless country, with their eventual goal of taking over the Middle East. For the Soviet interpretation, consider the following explanation released by Tass, the Soviet press agency, as to why 100,000 troops invaded Afghanistan.

The government of the Democratic Republic of Afghanistan, taking into account the continuing and broadening interference and provocations of external enemies of Afghanistan, and with a view to defending the gains of the April revolution, territorial integrity and national independence and maintaining peace and security, proceeding from the treaty of friendship, good neighborliness and cooperation of December 5, 1978, has approached the USSR with an insistent request for urgent political, moral and economic aid, including military aid, which the Democratic Republic of Afghanistan repeatedly requested from the government of the Soviet Union previously. The government of the Soviet Union has met the request of the Afghan side.

Compare this to an official explanation of the United States invasion of Vietnam, as stated by President Lyndon B. Johnson in 1964, after Congress overwhelmingly gave approval for "all necessary action to protect our armed forces" in Southeast Asia (Gulf of Tonkin Resolution):

As I have repeatedly made clear, the United States intends no rashness, and seeks no wider war. We must make it clear to all that the United States is united in its determination to bring about the end of Communist subversion and agression in the area.[3]

The crux of the problem of both countries—the Soviet Union and the United States—regarding Vietnam, Afghanistan, or any other political issue of contention is that each side believes their side to be correct. Yet this is the result of half-brained mentality, which is characteristic of all humans and not of just "Soviets" or "Americans." The problems between the Soviet Union and the United States (or between any countries at odds) are not going to be solved by "confronting" the issues, by conferences, summit meetings, or by war. Solutions will come only when half-brained people (us mere mortals) become whole-brained.

[3]Lyndon Johnson, *Mother Jones* (May 1980), p. 36.

Part Thinks It's Whole

When we use only a small percentage of our minds, there is a tendency to mistake a part of something for the whole. We see this happening every day, and at every level. A young woman may believe that saying "I do" will solve all of her problems. A young man may really think that all he needs to do is to add "M.D." after his last name and he will be in vacation condominiums and Mercedeses for the rest of his life. Parents may give their children lots of money, a car when they turn sixteen, and unlimited freedom and think all of their children's needs are met. But then they wonder why their kids get in trouble with the law.

This problem of seeing only the trees and not the forest has no room for intelligence. Because someone with an I.Q. of 150 is still only using one-fifth of his or her brain, it's not surprising to see this confined thinking even at the most advanced scientific levels. For example, when the anti-psychotic tranquilizers (Thorazine, Stelazine, etc.) first hit the pharmacies, the drugs were hailed as the cure for schizophrenia. Five years ago, lithium, a common salt, was being touted as a cure for manic-depression. Many medical doctors and psychiatrists firmly believe that mental illness is nothing but a chemical imbalance. On the other hand, behavioral psychologists believe that there is no such thing as mental illness and claim that emotional disorders are nothing but learned maladaptive behaviors. For them, treatment is easy—simply extinguish these behaviors. This mini-minded mentality leads these behavioral psychologists to try methods such as putting male homosexuals in a screening room and shocking them whenever a picture of a nude man is flashed on the screen. When they try to cure obesity, these behaviorists try to make overweight people vomit when they see food.

In his book, *The Mind Field*, Dr. Robert Ornstein draws our attention to the part-whole problem as it occurs at the scientific, psychological, and cultural levels:

> We are, I think, at a transition point: the beginning of the end of this adolescence. In many areas people are beginning to feel

90

that we have left something (without knowing what) out of our cultural upbringing, out of our science, medicine, education, and personal development. Perhaps we base too many of our plans on the assumption of social and material progress, an assumption rooted in the seemingly limitless growth of the past two generations.

Yet, even those people who are most concerned and interested in traditional approaches to human development still attempt to judge them with the stunted perspective of a contemporary ethnocentrism. Our 'no limits' culture provides the basis: The North American baseball championship for men is the 'World' Series. We may be informed by our television weather announcer that the 'all-time' record for rain or heat was set on a certain date: here, 'all-time' usually means the past hundred years. Our medical, educational, and scientific journals rarely refer to any fact or finding published before 1940 (with the exception of an obligatory honorific reference to Greece), and anything discovered or understood before the First World War is considered ancient history. In our approach to science and to consciousness, we bear the remnants of identifying our culture's specific developments with the sum total of knowledge and we attempt to measure some of the most important traditional human ideas on the scanty yardstick of our own habits of mind.[4]

In our approach to pressing social and cultural problems, our inability to get "The Wide Screen Video" is most characteristic and disabling. The failure of governments to deal with problems like crime, poverty, malnutrition, drug abuse, pollution, inept auto mechanics, and so forth is an example of this defect.

For every life problem, we have a separate governmental department. Poverty problems are handled by the Department of Health, Education and Welfare; nukes are handled by the Department of Energy; air and water pollution by the Environmental Protection Agency; crime by several agencies (depending, of course, on the type of crime commited); and so forth.

Setting up these separate governmental departments to deal with the varied ills of society is like trying to cure measles by painting over the spots. To cure measles, we need a *systemic* approach, which means instead of considering each of society's ills

[4]Robert Ornstein, *The Mind Field* (New York: Simon & Schuster/Pocket Books, 1976), pp. 21–22.

as separate problems, we will benefit by seeking the underlying causes—the thread that ties them all together.

"Accidental" Coincidence

It is very easy for us to consider coincidences as purely accidental or random happenstance. Scientists, especially, cling to this idea and brainwash us into believing it.

But the idea of chance coincidence is merely an assumption. An alternative assumption is to consider coincidental happenings as more than just coincidental—as the possible reflection of something broader. Instead of the idea of coincidence (which implies randomness), a newer idea, referred to as *synchronicity*, can be invoked. This term was first coined by the Swiss psychoanalyst Carl Jung to refer to "meaningful coincidence without apparent cause." Using this idea of synchronicity, several writers have since expanded on the concept and new ways of thinking about reality have emerged. Two such books are: *The Roots of Coincidence* (New York: Random House, 1972) by Arthur Koestler, and *The Challenge of Chance* (New York: Random House, 1974) by Sir Alister Hardy, Robert Harvie, and Arthur Koestler.

Probably the best book on the subject is Alan Vaughan's *Incredible Coincidence*. In it he documents 150 actual cases, all of which are indeed incredible. These include (in capsule form):

- A German housewife discovers the ring she lost forty years earlier—inside a potato.
- Frederick Chance crashes into Frederick Chance.
- A lead coffin is swept out to sea by a hurricane and floats two thousand miles—home.
- Two men trying to cash a forged, stolen check ended up in jail after they came face to face with their intended victim at the teller's window of an Austin (Texas) bank.
- Author Alan Vaughan gave a lecture in 1974 in Monterey, California. The next morning, becoming impatient with the bus service, he hitchhiked. The first car that came by picked him up. It was a woman who had attended his lecture and her name was Mrs. Allen who lived on Vaughan Road. Further, Mr. Vaughan was headed for the San Carlos Hotel and so was Mrs. Allen who was on her way there for a wedding reception.

• A bullet finds its deadly mark twenty years after it is fired—by chance.[5]

In this last example dating from 1893, Henry Ziegland, of Honey Grove, Texas jilted his sweetheart, who then killed herself. Her brother tried to avenge her by shooting Ziegland, but the bullet grazed his face and went into a nearby tree. The brother, believing he had killed Ziegland, committed suicide. In 1913, Ziegland was having trouble cutting down the tree with the bullet in it, so he used dynamite, and the explosion sent the old bullet through his head—killing him.

In the process of describing these 150 examples of synchronicity, Vaughan adds commentary and other sidelights, all of which recommend that the reader pay greater attention to the coincidences in everyday life. One will then begin to realize the possibility that something of wider significance may be happening.

Vaughan speculates that synchronicity or "meaningful coincidences" might be choreographed by our unconscious minds—our shared, collective unconscious. The implication is that psychic interconnections link us all with one another (and with everything else), beyond the conventions of space and time.

This may all be so. Certainly the experience of synchronicity in our daily lives can expand our awareness and suggest to us the idea of something greater—an overriding pattern—the bigger picture.

Tunnel Vision

We all get touches of this block to seeing "The Big Picture" on a daily basis; in fact, some would venture to say it has reached epidemic proportions in twentieth century man and woman. The disease? *Tunnel Vision*, the self-imposed process of restriction that serves to narrow one's interests, understanding or perception. It is subconscious parochialism in everyday life.

Tunnel vision is most visible in experts or specialists (even though all of us have it). Frequently, experts or specialists can't

[5]Alan Vaughan, *Incredible Coincidence* (New York: Harper & Row, Pub., 1979), p. 1; p. 27.

think of anything else but their own area of expertise—they view all of life through their little "tunnel." They know so much about their subject that they know close to nothing about anything else.

Examples, like rampant cases of tunnel vision, abound. The economist, to name one expert, who judges virtually everything according to dollars and cents—he has dollar signs in his pupils. The dog breeder is another example. She may know everything about one particular breed of dog and very little about dogs in general. Her home is filled with dog magazines, dog encyclopedias, show calendars, ribbons, photographs, dog food, and so on. And, most interestingly, the dog breeder usually looks like a particular hound.

Sports enthusiasts are also major offenders (sports "fan" is, after all, short for "fanatic"). The sports enthusiast lunges for the morning paper and tears through stories about earthquakes, elections, major legislation, the economy, and even the comics until he (usually they *are* male) gets to the sports page. He can usually rattle off scores and names of players from decades past, but has trouble remembering who ran in the 1976 presidential election.

Another group of tunnel vision patients are the coupon clippers; most often, these are avid homemakers. The coupon hoarders are a breed apart. They spend up to forty hours a week clipping, trading, and filing coupons. They start clubs and networks going. They spend another ten or twenty hours a week driving all over town, looking for these bargains. Then they pride themselves on saving $50 to $75 a week on their grocery bills. It probably never occurs to them that their coupon compulsion is actually *costing* them money: for a fifty-hour work week, they are earning about half the current minimum wage.

Similar manias afflict people in many areas of life—body builders, nutrition nuts, joggers, tennis players, culinary experts, television addicts (vidiots), car freaks (gearheads), stereo aficionados, and so on.

Unfortunately, tunnel vision has no respect for intelligence. The more intelligent the person, the more likely he or she is to be afflicted with tunnel vision. Professors, scientists, doctors, and academicians are especially prone. The historian knows all about history, or narrows his expertise to one specific period of history.

Ask him to step into the present and discuss biology, fashion, music, or anything and he will either stare at you blankly or try to give you a historical perspective on those subjects ("Today's fashions are really a throwback to post World War II Germany, when...")。 Even within their narrow range of interest, scholars tend to be terribly biased. Many of them even have a pet theory that denounces the existence of anything else.

The field of psychology is an especially good example. Academic psychologists have their area of specialization very narrowly delineated. You should never try to learn about cognitive brain theory from an expert in sexual dysfunction. There are academic psychologists who specialize in nonsense syllables, while others' area of expertise is short-term memory (as opposed to long-term memory), sensory deprivation, massed learning (as opposed to spaced learning), perceptual defense (as opposed to perceptual vigilance), rat learning (as opposed to pigeons, maybe...?), and so on.

In clinical psychology, an area supposedly devoted to sound mental functioning, the situation is also quite narrow and short-sighted. In a field where there are at least three dozen major schools of thought, all of which (and none of which) have some validity, the majority of practitioners hold to only *one* of these approaches to the exclusion of all the rest. Probably because it's less confusing to the psychologist.

For example, the Transactional Analyst sees all human inter-action in terms of "child, parent, or adult," or "I'm OK, you're OK." The Psychoanalyst talks very little, is concerned with sex and dreams, id, ego, superego, and the past. The Gestaltist and Reality Therapist dispense with the past. The Rational Therapist talks a lot, and is concerned with thinking and emotional control. The Behavior Therapist dispenses with experience, consciousness, and mind, while the Transpersonal Therapist does the opposite. Psy-chiatrists have a different drug for every different type of patient, while the psychologist discourages drugs. Try inviting one of each to a dinner party for some *real* action.

Close-mindedness and obsession, then, become more charac-teristic of the therapists than of the patients they treat. Abraham Maslow, perhaps one of the more open-minded psychology spokesmen, once stated that if the only tool you have is a hammer, you will treat everything like a nail. "Hammer head" is not a name reserved exclusively to a kind of shark.

Obsessions and *compulsions* are a form of tunnel vision. An obsession is a thought or view that dominates a person's mind ("white bread is the *only* kind of bread to serve bologna on..."), while a compulsion is an activity that a person cannot help but do. (We all know people who are compulsive cleaners.) The obsessive cannot think otherwise, while the compulsive cannot do otherwise. And most normal folk tend to exhibit these characteristics at one time or another.

Someone who holds to one religion, with the total exclusion of any other truths found in other faiths is obsessed. Someone who thinks their brand or product (car, toothpaste, deodorant, and so on) is "best" is obsessed. Nationalism is a form of obsession. Americans tend to think their country is the best; Canadians think their nation is tops.

Many well-known leaders in their fields tend to be obsessed, as are their followers. Examples abound, but since we're talking about psychology, let's consider a leader in the field of psychology. B.F. Skinner is a psychologist who used to be a major force in his field (particularly in the sixties), and to this day, is held in a position of high regard. He pioneered the behavioristic school of thought, which holds that behavior or action is fundamental (if not exclusively so) in animal and human functioning. Skinner's views are taught in every major university psychology department throughout the world; he is somewhat of a celebrity—sought after for speaking engagements and well known for his behavioristic bible, *Walden Two* (New York: Macmillan, 1949, 1968). He invented the Skinner Box, a type of cage wherein rats and pigeons peck at levers for food. In fact, his daughter was raised in a modified version of the box. Skinner is such a believer in his theory of behaviorism that at one time, he used to keep cumulative records and graphs of his own writing behavior.

Skinner, then, is obsessed with behavior. Behavior is his God; he denies the importance (and perhaps even the existence) of mind, consciousness, and experience. His world is a behavioral one. Emotion is "expressive" behavior; thought is "subverbal vocalization;" perception is "sensory response;" "mind," "will," "dreams," "images," and "feelings" are merely "ghosts in the machine."

So, it is easy to see that psychogenic provincialism is an open trap, waiting to catch us. We must be aware of our tendency to wear blinders. A good way to test ourselves is to see how many issues or problems facing us in our daily world we tend to look at in terms of black and white. Do we see only one way that these issues or problems can be resolved? Or do we see the gray areas? Another way to test ourselves is to notice how much we know about the world around us. Do we know what's going on in the fields of music, drama, literature, medicine, or technology? Do we know what our politicians are up to? How about energy, foreign affairs, the environment?

When we become aware of these stumbling blocks—the biases, the tunnel vision and so forth—to holistic, comprehensive thinking, we have taken the first step in expanding our consciousness. Thus, we can begin to see The Big Picture.

chapter eleven
YOUR INTUITION KNOWS

Katherine was a bright, young writer at a fairly large magazine. She was offered a high-paying, glamorous position with a relatively new advertising agency that boasted an impressive array of national accounts. The agency had a good reputation in town; the employees were all energetic and success-oriented. However, something told Katherine to hold up on her decision. She told the agency she would possibly be ready to make a move six months down the line. Within three months, the agency had folded.

Bob met a young woman who had everything he was looking for in the perfect mate. She was attractive, personable, intelligent, and had a good career. Though his acquaintances and friends kept teasing him about "when he was going to pop the question," Bob could not visualize their being together. Something just wasn't right. A year later, the woman was convicted of embezzlement.

Nancy worked at a large insurance agency. One particular day, she noticed that she had lost her favorite gold bracelet. Since she had been in and out of the office during the day, she could have lost it in any conceivable place. However, she decided to ask a few people in the office if they had seen her bracelet. After receiving several negative answers, she impulsively asked a woman in the office with whom she rarely spoke if she had seen the bracelet. The woman had, and was about to turn it over to the manager of the firm.

Strange, how these people just *knew* what to do. And their knowledge certainly wasn't based on annual reports, computerized compatibility charts, or the use of metal detectors. They *knew* because they listened to those subtle little voices, if you will, within them that said, "Do this!" or "Wait this one out..."

Though the word *intuition* for some may conjure up visions of psychics running around in flowing caftans, steaming up their crystal balls, intuition does exist even in the most rational, logical, and conventional of minds. It's that sixth sense, that faculty of the mind that operates independently of reason and logic. It's a way of knowing or sensing something that produces instantaneous comprehension. And, like sagging muscles, it can be developed with the aid of a bit of practice.

The process of intuition, "the hunching skill," is best described by the author, Max Gunther, in his book *The Luck Factor*:

> A hunch is a conclusion that is based on perfectly real data—on objective facts that have been accurately observed, efficiently sorted, logically processed in your mind. The facts on which the hunch is based, however, are *facts you don't consciously know*. They are stored and processed on some level of awareness just below or behind the conscious level. This is why a hunch comes with that peculiar feeling of almost-but-not-quite-knowing. It is something that you think you know, but you don't know how you know it.[1]

So, you say to yourself smugly, if everyone has this so-called intuition, how do we put it to work? Well, maybe intuition won't help you balance your checkbook or win an upcoming debate tourney, but give this hunching skill a chance. Business decisions are not always based on the computer printouts that stare you glumly in the eye. You must have a "feel" for what will be most profitable. Having a nice romance is not all based on those well-intentioned articles written up in the latest women's magazines. You must "sense" what is right between you and the object of your desires. Finding a lost pet does not mean only going down the alleys and past the fire hydrants you usually walk Fido by. You must be able to "know" which backyard to peer in; which strange street to turn down.

[1] Max Gunther, *The Luck Factor* (New York: Macmillan, 1977), p. 125.

Enough for the case of intuition?

And now, a few do's and don'ts about the process of intuition before we plunge into the nittier and grittier aspects of how to develop this orphaned faculty:

1. Intuitive experiences occur spontaneously. When you least expect it, you're elected ... and so on. You cannot *make* them happen ("Okay, now I have to decide whether I should take this job in Hoboken ... I'll make my intuition work ... Okay, work intuition! Work!"), but you can—and should—recognize them when they occur.
2. Certain qualities make you more sensitive to intuitive experiences, like relaxation (those little voices don't like terminally tense people), patience (ditto for those who want instant gratification), humility, and self-control.
3. Intuition should not be confused with hope. Just because you hope so hard that you get that high-paying, high-stress job, doesn't mean it will happen.
4. Intuition is developed through trial and error. Through trial and error you should learn to distinguish it from hope, fear, impulsiveness, and fantasy.
5. Intuition is not emotion or intellect.
6. And here's the clincher: Intuition cannot be explained. You *know* when you've got it.

Here are four additional tips for training intuition:

1. Learn to tune into intuitive experiences; to recognize their quality. Their quality is unique and can be distinguished from intellection and emotion. Intuitive impulses are a form of perception—they are sensed. They are distinguished by a vague sensation of being "certain" or (more commonly) "almost certain."
2. Be aware of "soft" facts as well as "hard" ones. Hard facts are logical, objective, overt—the kind we tend to associate with lawyers and news reporters. Soft facts are less formal or obvious, such as impressions, feelings, inclinations, and vibrations. In most situations, both hard and soft facts will reveal themselves. For example, the boss of a large company was absent from the last staff meeting and asked his secretary and his male assistant what transpired. His assistant reports: "Everyone was present ... we discussed the East Side construction project, its cost, labor problems ... we are behind schedule." His secretary reports: "Bill and Joe seemed uptight ... there was a chill in the air ... I could sense they were at odds and Bill was about to explode when ... I felt

quite uneasy until..." "Hard facts are obvious, conscious, tangible; soft facts are hunches, intuitive, invisible."[2]

3. Intuition is commonly experienced within the context of choice. When a choice needs to be made, intuition will signal stop or go. This faculty or function is developed by comparison and contrast. By comparing your subjective experience with the eventual correctness or incorrectness of your choice, you can eventually sense the impression which will match-up.

4. Be true to your intuition. Extraneous factors will often intrude, such as social pressures, wish fulfillment, greed, impatience, and so on, which can alter the basis for your decision.

This is not to say that these pointers will help everyone develop their intuition; they are simply a guide for what you must do for yourself. There are no recipes, no magic chants to awaken that "sleeping genius" within you. You must do it yourself.

Another word of caution: do not bounce around your daily world exclaiming, "my intuition tells me that..." every five minutes. Don't rely solely upon it; study the situation, use the other side of your brain, too. Research. After you've done your research, then let intuition guide you to your final choice. Intuition is something to use in conjunction with your logical, rational abilities.

Because of cultural and educational emphasis upon logical thinking and rational analysis, we have ignored our normal intuitive abilities to such an extent that people we meet who rely upon their intuition will amaze us.

NUTS

A cat said to a squirrel:
'How wonderful it is that you can so unerringly locate buried nuts, to nurture you through the winter!'

The squirrel said:
'What, to a squirrel, would be remarkable would be a squirrel who was *unable* to do such things!'[3]

[2]Ibid., pp. 139–40.
[3]Idries Shah, "Nuts," *The Magic Monastery* (London: Jonathan Cape, 1972), p. 41.

Yet, this is ordinary intuition. Beyond that, we have the potential to develop an even greater form of intuition. The psychiatrist and author, Dr. Arthur Deikman, writing on "Sufism and Psychiatry" points out that, "Ordinary intuition, however, is considered by the Sufis to be a lower-level imitation of the superior form of intuition with which Sufism is concerned."[4]

This superior form is what is referred to in Eastern and Western spiritual traditions as cosmic intuition; a state of enlightenment connected with the perception of "ultimate truth." An example deriving from this superior form of intuition is given here.

THE ATOM

Crack the heart of any atom: from its midst you will see a sun shining. If you give all you have to Love, I'll be called a Pagan if you suffer a molecule of loss. The soul passed through the fire of Love will let you see the soul transmuted. If you escape the narrowness of dimensions, and will see the 'time of what is placeless', you will hear what has never been heard, and you will see what has never been seen; until they deliver you to a place where you will see 'a world' and 'worlds' as one. You shall love Unity with heart and soul; until with the true eye, you will see Unity...[5]

—Sayed Ahmad Hatif

[4]Arthur Deikman, "Sufism and Psychiatry," *Journal of Nervous and Mental Disease*, 165, no. 5, 1977, p. 322.
[5]Idries Shah, "The Atom," *The Way of the Sufi* (New York: Dutton, 1970), p. 245.

chapter twelve
DREAM LIFE

It happens time and again. The young woman is dressed in full bridal regalia. She begins to march down the aisle. The church pews are full—everyone she knows is there. Suddenly, it occurs to her that she's not entirely sure of exactly who it is she is marrying. She gets nearer to the altar. The dark-haired groom turns around. His face is blank; featureless. The young woman jolts awake from the dream.

We sleep one-third of our total life—that's about twenty-five years of the average lifespan. According to modern research, it is estimated that we dream 20% of the time we are asleep—about five full years out of our life.

Dream research bases this 20% estimate on the finding that during light sleep, we tend to recall our dreams most easily and that these recalled dreams correspond with what the researchers refer to as the REM period (rapid eye movement—rapid back-and-forth movements of the eyes, which are measured through closed lids). But this doesn't necessarily mean we aren't dreaming during periods of deeper sleep. In fact, when REMs aren't noticeable, there is evidence that significant mental activity occurs in deep sleep as well. Edgar Allen Poe, for example, suggested that we are probably constantly dreaming during sleep, and tend to only recall dreams that occur in the lighter phases. In his words, every time we awaken "we break the thread of some dream."

Other thinkers and writers have even claimed we dream almost *all the time*, even when we are awake. P.D. Ouspensky, the Russian philosopher, after careful study of himself and others for over thirty years, boldly stated:

> It is not at all necessary to be asleep in order to observe dreams. Dreams never stop. We do not notice them in a waking state, amidst the continuous flow of visual, auditory and other sensations, for the same reason for which we do not see stars in the light of the sun. But just as we can see the stars from the bottom of a deep well, so we can see the dreams which go on in us if, even for a short time, we isolate ourselves whether accidentally or intentionally, from the inflow of external impressions ... and with astonishment you suddenly see yourself surrounded by a strange world of shadows, moods, conversations, sounds, pictures. And you understand then that this world is always in you, that it never disappears.[1]

Certain contemporary dream experts have discovered that most dreams tend to reflect our private lives and our innermost conflicts—conflicts relating to freedom and security, love and hate, right and wrong, life and death, success and failure, hope and fear. In this interpretation, by understanding our dreams we can better understand ourselves—our deeper, underlying selves. Who knows what evil lurks in the hearts of men? The dream knows. In the dream, it

> ... is revealed how the person truly sees himself when he has stripped off his waking pretenses, how he sees people and the pressures of his environment, how he perceives his impulses and wishes and the moral conflicts they all create.[2]

Contemporary experts on dream interpretation tend to reject the once-popular Freudian views about dreams, in that they don't accept the idea that most dreams are purely symbolic of something else—that something else having to do with sexual gratification and erotic conflict only (tunnels, approaching trains, snakes, and so on).

[1]P.D. Ouspensky, *A New Model of the Universe* (New York: Random House/Vintage, 1971), pp. 263–64.
[2]Faye Hammel and Daniel Marshall, *The Dream Theatre* (New York: Harper & Row, Pub., 1978), p. 5.

It is admitted that many dreams speak to us in a special language—the language of symbols, parables, allegories, paradox, and riddles. But these are now considered as being directly representative of ongoing problems, conflicts, hopes, and fears relative to our everyday existence.

As an example, in her excellent book, *The Dream Game*, Dr. Ann Faraday relates a recurring dream told her by a university lecturer in which he is walking through the college grounds or reading in the library, when he suddenly notices all eyes upon him, and looking down realizes he is stark naked, clad only in shoes and socks. After discussing the dream with him, Faraday realized that the dream reflected a deep-rooted fear of his—that of being exposed. He admitted to her that his writings and lectures were mainly compiled from works and ideas of other people and that he had the constant fear of being exposed. Faraday suggested to him that the dream would probably tend to repeat itself until he either changed his approach or resolved his inner conflict in some other way.[3]

An outstanding feature of dreams, besides their commonly bizarre nature, is that they tend to transcend the usual boundaries of logic and linear time. Dreams are the ultimate in nonlinear thinking. In his book, *Dream Psychology*, the late Dr. Maurice Nicoll noted that dreams are like cartoons; pictorial images, often funny, which break our patterns of conventional thinking, tie together a great deal in one or two captions, and—when understood—add insight.

As an example, he related a dream in which he was staying at a large hotel that resembled a cathedral, and was greeted by the manager, who was a priest, and who was carrying a dinner bell. Upon examination, Nicoll was able to connect this simple dream with a whole collection of events and people from his past; the headmaster of a religious school who had made an impression upon him, the dinner bell that was used to signal mealtime at home, and a series of other intertwined associations running throughout his life up to the current time of the dream, when he had an interest in the then well-known Cardinal Newman.[4]

[3]Ann Faraday, *The Dream Game* (New York: Harper & Row, Pub., 1976), p. 73.
[4]Maurice Nicoll, *Dream Psychology* (New York: Samuel Weiser, 1979), pp. 27–32.

Dreams then, are often characterized by their ability to compress great amounts of information, facts and impressions in a quick succession of time. They have a simultaneous, holistic quality, which, once understood, allows us to better appreciate the remarkable powers of our minds.

Since most of us pay little attention to our dreams as a way to make better use of our minds—to get more from our brains—it would profit us to learn more about our dreams, to record and study them.

You can record your dreams in a note pad kept near your bed or by tape recorder. Before going to sleep remind yourself that you are going to dream and that upon awakening (whenever that may be) you will remember everything. Upon awakening, don't jolt up quickly (as this may interfere with recall), but lie there momentarily, reviewing the details of the dream. Then write down as much as you can (not trying *too* hard), and simultaneously record how you feel at the moment or how you felt in the dream. You can transcribe your dreams more neatly during the day (or before retiring at night) in a dream journal. Drawing pictures or adding comments is sometimes also helpful.

With practice, you should get better and better. In order to enhance the effect, avoid sleeping pills as they reduce REM activity. Faye Hammel and Daniel Marshall in their manual, *The Dream Theatre*, note there may be ways to enhance dream recall: "Henry Reed, the editor of *Sundance Community Dream Journal*, suggests the Tibetan technique of focusing the desire for dreams into a concentrated 'glow' in the back of the throat. One psychiatrist advises taking Vitamin B-6, while Amanda Tree, a New York herbologist, claims that sleeping on a pillow stuffed with mugwort, yarrow, and Foti-tieng increases dream recall."[5]

Another important aspect of dreams, besides their personal quality, is that (and this has been noticed by thinkers throughout history) they have common themes that men and women from all times and places share. The great psychoanalyst, Carl Jung, referred to these commonly-shared themes as reflections of *archetypes:* "mental forces whose presence cannot be explained by

[5]Hammel and Marshall, *The Dream Theatre*, p. 5.

anything in the individual's own life and which seem to be aboriginal, innate, and inherited shapes of the human mind."⁶ He believed such archetypes were representative of the most fundamental need or goal of humanity—to self-develop and to strive for insight into the spiritual and celestial nature of the universe.

Interestingly enough, archetypal dreams share the same features found in fairy tales—those fascinating and mysterious stories of ancient lore shared in one related form or another among all cultures. Such features are documented in all the well-known collections, such as those of Hans Christian Anderson, the Brothers Grimm, Perrault, Staropola, Boccaccio, Chaucer, Shakespeare, and others. In a recent collection, compiled by Idries Shah under the title of *World Tales*, Shah notes in the Introduction:

> Many traditional tales have a surface meaning (perhaps just a socially uplifting one) and a secondary, inner significance, which is rarely glimpsed consciously, but which nevertheless acts powerfully upon our minds. Tales have always been used, so far as we can judge, for spiritual as well as social pruposes: and as parables with more or less obvious meanings this use is familiar to most people today. But as Professor Geoffrey Parrinder says of the myth, 'its inner truth was realized when the participant was transported into the realm of the sacred and eternal.'

> Perhaps above all the tale fulfills the function not of escape but of hope. The suspending of ordinary constraints helps people to reclaim optimism and to fuel the imagination with energy for the attainment of goals; whether moral or material. Maxim Gorky realized this when he wrote: 'In tales people fly through the air on magic carpets, walk in seven-league boots, build castles overnight; the tales opened up for me a new world where some free and all-fearless power reigned and inspired in me a dream of a better life.'⁷

The following tale, "The Algonquin Cinderella," well illustrates the "function not of escape but hope," which could just as easily be a dream shared by every one of us, always and everywhere. First, Idries Shah's introduction to the tale:

⁶Ibid., p. 2.
⁷Idries Shah, *World Tales* (New York: Harcourt Brace Jovanovich, 1979), p. *vii*.

At the end of the last century, Mrs. M. R. Cox collected three hundred years of Cinderella-type stories. They totalled 345 versions: and she added that they could be multiplied. This may be one of the most enduring of all tales—a variety has been noted (by Arthur Waley) in a Chinese book of the ninth century A.D. My father published a Vietnamese variant, claimed to be a thousand years old, in 1960. It has also been observed that the story of Aslaug, daughter of Siegfried and Brunhild in the Volsung Saga, is a striking parallel. Apart from the now-popular version of Perrault, published in the 18th century, there are other intriguing and excellent tales featuring the pathetic Cinders. Of these, the Scottish variant is 'Rashin Coatie'—Coat of Rushes—and there is an English one: 'Cap o' Rushes.' People have argued about the slipper—should it have been glass or fur. Children love the details of the ball, the magic pumpkin, the wicked stepmother, and why should they not? But for sheer beauty and delight, this American version, found among the Algonquin Indians, seems hard to beat.

THE ALGONQUIN CINDERELLA

There was once a large village of the MicMac Indians of the Eastern Algonquins built beside a lake. At the far end of the settlement stood a lodge, and in it lived a being who was always invisible. He had a sister who looked after him, and everyone knew that any girl who could see him might marry him. For that reason there were very few girls who did not try, but it was very long before anyone succeeded.

This is the way in which the test of sight was carried out: at evening-time, when the Invisible One was due to be returning home, his sister would walk with any girl who might come down to the lakeshore. She, of course, could see her brother, since he was always visible to her. As soon as she saw him, she would say to the girls:

"Do you see my brother?"

"Yes," they would generally reply—though some of them did say "No."

To those who said that they could indeed see him, the sister would say:

"Of what is his shoulder strap made?" Some people say that she would enquire:

"What is his moose-runner's haul?" or "With what does he draw his sled?"

And they would answer:

"A strip of rawhide" or "a green flexible branch," or something of that kind.

Then she, knowing that they had not told the truth, would say:

"Very well, let us return to the wigwam!"

When they had gone in, she would tell them not to sit in a certain place, because it belonged to the Invisible One. Then, after they had helped to cook the supper, they would wait with great curiosity, to see him eat. They could be sure that he was a real person, for when he took off his moccasins they became visible, and his sister hung them up. But beyond this they saw nothing of him, not even when they stayed in the place all the night, as many of them did.

Now there lived in the village an old man who was a widower, and his three daughters. The youngest girl was very small, weak and often ill: and yet her sisters, especially the elder, treated her cruelly. The second daughter was kinder, and sometimes took her side: but the wicked sister would burn her hands and feet with hot cinders, and she was covered with scars from this treatment. She was so marked that people called her Oochigeaskw, the Rough-Faced Girl.

When her father came home and asked why she had such burns, the bad sister would at once say that it was her own fault, for she had disobeyed orders and gone near the fire and fallen into it.

These two elder sisters decided one day to try their luck at seeing the Invisible One. So they dressed themselves in their finest clothes, and tried to look their prettiest. They found the Invisible One's sister and took the usual walk by the water.

When he came, and when they were asked if they could see him, they answered: "Of course." And when asked about the shoulder strap or sled cord, they answered: "A piece of rawhide."

But of course they were lying like the others, and they got nothing for their pains.

The next afternoon, when the father returned home, he brought with him many of the pretty little shells from which wampum was made, and they set to work to string them.

That day, poor little Oochigeaskw, who had always gone barefoot, got a pair of her father's moccasins, old ones, and put them into water to soften them so that she could wear them. Then she begged her sisters for a few wampum shells. The elder called her a "little pest," but the younger one gave her some. Now, with no other clothes than her usual rags, the poor little thing went into the woods and got herself some sheets of birch bark, from which she made a dress, and put marks on it for decoration, in the style of long ago. She made a petticoat and a loose gown, a cap, leggings and a hand-kerchief. She put on her father's large old moccasins, which were far too big for her, and went forth to try her luck. She would try, she thought, to discover whether she could see the Invisible One.

She did not begin very well. As she set off, her sisters shouted and hooted, hissed and yelled, and tried to make her stay. And the loafers around the village seeing the strange little creature, called out "Shame!"

The poor little girl in her strange clothes, with her face all scarred, was an awful sight, but she was kindly received by the sister of the Invisible One. And this was, of course, because this noble lady understood far more about things than simply the mere outside which all the rest of the world knows. As the brown of the evening sky turned to black, the lady took her down to the lake.

"Do you see him?" the Invisible One's sister asked.

"I do, indeed—and he is wonderful!" said Oochigeaskw.

The sister asked:

"And what is his sled-string?"

The little girl said:

"It is the Rainbow."

"And, my sister, what is his bow-string?"

"It is The Spirit's Road—the Milky Way."

"So you have seen him," said his sister. She took the girl home with her and bathed her. As she did so, all the scars disappeared from her body. Her hair grew again, as it was combed, long, like a blackbird's wing. Her eyes were now like stars: in all the world there was no other such beauty. Then, from her treasures, the lady gave her a wedding garment and adorned her.

Then she told Oochigeaskw to take the wife's seat in the wigwam: the one next to where the Invisible One sat, beside the entrance. And when he came in, terrible and beautiful, he smiled and said:

"So we are found out!"

"Yes," said his sister. And so Oochigeaskw became his wife.[8]

---

[8]Ibid, pp. 152–55

chapter thirteen
A MULTI-I.Q. SYSTEM

Yogurt is made by adding a small quantity of old yogurt to a larger portion of milk. The action of *bacillus bulgaricus* in the seeding portion of the yogurt will in time convert the whole into a mass of new yogurt.

> One day some friends saw Nasrudin down on his knees beside a pond. He was adding a little old yogurt to the water. One of the men said,
>
> "What are you trying to do, Nasrudin?"
>
> "I am trying to make yogurt."
>
> "But you can't make yogurt in that way!"
>
> "Yes, I know; but just *supposing* it takes!"[1]

Almost anyone will smile at the idiocy of the ignorant Mulla, yet there are among us many so-called "experts" who would suggest we can achieve expanded brain power with equally futile methods. Books with titles like *Mind Games, The Book of Highs, Total Mind Power,* and others offer exercises and activities such as these:

"You should do a half hour to a full hour's worth of stomach-to-floor crawling every day during your three-week brain boost,

[1] Idries Shah, *The Sufis* (New York: Doubleday/Anchor, 1964), p. 101.

111

broken up into five ten-minute sessions scattered throughout the day. For some people, this is the hardest step in brain-building."[2]

Another highly touted way to heighten your awareness and perception is presented by Nicholas Regush and June Regush, authors of *The New Consciousness Catalogue*, who suggest "The Drum":

> An Optokinetic Perceptual Learning Device for Stimulating Sensory Awareness and Learning.
>
> Invented by psychologist Eleanor Criswell, the drum makes use of reflex eye movements. Your eyes follow the drum as it goes round and round, and they react to the patterns of its design as well as to the reflection of light from the drum's surface.[3]

It's supposed benefit—"a higher level of brain functioning." In the text, along with their description of the "Drum," the authors issue a warning that this "tool" is not for casual use, and requires the assistance of an expert in the field.

Another book commands you to "stop reading and go stand on your head for five minutes or do a shoulder stand," telling the reader this is an excellent way to alter consciousness.

"Postures are body gestures, positions, sometimes natural, sometimes contained, into which we can arrange our bodies. Postures help us to become our bodies, to become ourselves."[4]

Although these are just a few of the exercises presented in these modern "mind guides" (and admittedly, these are some of the more ridiculous suggestions), there is actually very little nutritional value in terms of real mind or brain expansion that can be found in any of these books or courses. This is because most of the authors' approaches are merely based on assumptions and guesswork, with "face validity" as their only basis.

Now let's go back to the tale of Nasrudin and the yogurt. It is part of an extensive collection of Sufi teaching stories, or "oral

---

[2]W. Wenger, *How to Increase Your Intelligence* (New York: Bobbs-Merrill, 1975), p. 77.

[3]Nicholas Regush and June Regush, *The New Consciousness Catalogue* (New York: Putnam's, 1979), p. 60.

[4]Edward Rosenfeld, *The Book of Highs* (New York: Quadrangle, 1973), p. 67.

literature" introduced by Idries Shah. In the past sixteen years, Shah has authored twenty-five books published in 150 editions in fifteen languages. In addition to teaching stories, his books contain a wide range of diverse materials: psychological exercises, meditations, proverbs, contemplation themes, narratives, aphorisms, humor, timely information, and social commentary.

Although this literary wisdom was created many centuries ago, some have seen a current need to take the essence of the Sufi's esoteric knowledge and transplant it into our contemporary society (such as one carrying a seed from a long dormant stock and planting it anew in freshly tilled soil). The effect will differ because our minds and souls deal with different kinds of environments and problems, but the end result will be a true expansion of our mental capacities.

Let's consider the following tale:

THE GNAT NAMOUSS—AND THE ELEPHANT

Once upon a time there was a gnat. His name was Namouss, and he was known, because of his sensitivity, as Perceptive Namouss. Namouss decided, after reflection upon his state, and for good and sufficient reasons, to move house. The place which he chose as eminently suitable was the ear of a certain elephant.

All that remained to do was to make the move, and quite soon Namouss had installed himself in the large and highly attractive quarters. Time passed. The gnat reared several families of gnatlets, and he sent them out into the world. As the years rolled past, he knew the usual moments of tension and relaxation, the feelings of joy and sorrow, of questing and achievement, which are the lot of the gnat wherever he may be found.

The elephant's ear was his home; and, as is always the case, he felt (and the feeling persisted until it became quite permanent) that there was a close connection between his life, his history, his very being and this place. The ear was so warm, so welcoming, so vast, the scene of so many experiences.

Naturally Namouss had not moved into the house without due ceremony and a regard for the proper observances of the situation. On the very first day, just before moving in, he had cried, at the top of his tiny voice, his decision. "O Elephant!"—

he had shouted—"Know that none other than I, Namouss the Gnat, known as Perceptive Namouss, propose to make this place my abode. As it is your ear, I am giving you the customary notice of my intention."

The elephant had raised no objection.

But Namouss did not know that the elephant had not heard him at all. Neither, for that matter, had his host felt the entry (or even the presence and absence) of the gnat and his various families. Not to labour the point unduly, he had no idea that the gnats were there at all.

And when the time came when Namouss the Perceptive decided, for what were to him compelling and important reasons, that he would move house again, he reflected that he must do so in accordance with established and hallowed custom. He prepared himself for the formal declaration of his abandonment of the Elephant's Ear.

Thus it was that, the decision finally and irrevocably taken and his words sufficiently rehearsed, Namouss shouted once more down the elephant's ear. He shouted once, and no answer came. He shouted again, and the elephant was still silent. The third time, gathering the whole strength of his voice in his determination to register his urgent yet eloquent words, he cried: "O Elephant! Know that I, the Gnat Perceptive Namouss, propose to leave my hearth and home, to quit my residence in this ear of yours where I have dwelt for so very long. And this is for a sufficient and significant reason which I am prepared to explain to you."

Now finally the words of the gnat came to the hearing of the elephant, and the gnat-cry penetrated. As the elephant pondered the words, Namouss shouted: "What have you to say in answer to my news? What are your feelings about my departure?"

The elephant raised his great head and trumpeted a little. And this trumpeting contained the sense: "Go in peace—for in truth your going is of as much interest and significance to me as was your coming."[5]

What was your reaction to the story? Were you puzzled? Were you able to put yourself in the gnat's place? In one sense, we are no

[5]Idries Shah, "The Gnat Namouss—and the Elephant," *Tales of the Dervishes* (New York: Dutton, 1970), pp. 58–59.

bigger than a gnat—(just change your frame of reference)—and also like the gnat in the story, we are often self-deceived. In a commentary accompanying the story, we are informed:

> The Tale of Perceptive Namouss might be taken at first glance as a sardonic illustration of a supposed uselessness of life. Such an interpretation, the Sufi would say, could only be due to the insensitivity of the reader.
>
> What is intended to be stressed here is the general lack of human judgment about the relative importance of things in life.
>
> Man thinks that important things are unimportant, and that trivial ones are vital.
>
> The story is attributed to Sheikh Hamza Malamati Maqtul. He organized the Malamatis and was executed in 1575, alleged to be a Christian.[6]

In Sufi stories, the elephant is sometimes symbolic of the wider significance of life. The "elephant" is perceived once self-deception ceases and broader awareness takes effect.

THE BLIND ONES AND THE MATTER OF THE ELEPHANT

Beyond Ghor there was a city. All its inhabitants were blind. A king with his entourage arrived near by; he brought his army and camped in the desert. He had a mighty elephant, which he used in attack and to increase the people's awe.

The populace became anxious to see the elephant, and some sightless from among this blind community ran like fools to find it.

As they did not even know the form or shape of the elephant, they groped sightlessly, gathering information by touching some part of it.

Each thought that he knew something, because he could feel a part.

When they returned to their fellow-citizens, eager groups clustered around them. Each of these was anxious, misguidedly, to learn the truth from those who were themselves astray.

[6]Ibid., pp. 59–60.

They asked about the form, the shape of the elephant: and listened to all they were told.

The man whose hand had reached an ear was asked about the elephant's nature. He said: "It is a large, rough thing, wide and broad, like a rug."

And the one who had felt the trunk said: "I have the real facts about it. It is like a straight and hollow pipe, awful and destructive."

The one who had felt its feet and legs said: "It is mighty and firm, like a pillar."

Each had felt one part out of many. Each had perceived it wrongly. No mind knew all: Knowledge is not the companion of the blind. All imagined something, something incorrect.

The created is not informed about divinity.There is no Way in this science by means of the ordinary intellect.[7]

Following is Idries Shah's commentary on this tale.

This tale is more famous in Rumi's version—"The Elephant in the Dark House," found in the *Mathnavi*. Rumi's teacher Hakim Sanai gives this earlier treatment in the first book of his Sufi classic *The Walled Garden of Truth*. He died in 1150.

Both stories are themselves renderings of a similar argument which, according to tradition, has been used by Sufi teaching masters for many centuries.[8]

The Sufis were aware we used only a small percentage of our total brain long before modern brain research came across this "discovery." In Sufi literature, as far back as 1000 years ago, humankind has been described as "blind," "asleep," and "unconscious." We are also described as "lame," "dumb," and "deaf." Idries Shah provides the following commentary:

It is related that the great Abdul-Qadir left a patched Sufi cloak to be presented to a successor to his mantle who was to be born nearly six hundred years after his death.

[7]Ibid., p. 25.
[8]Ibid., p. 26.

In 1563 Sayed Sikandar Shah, Qadiri, having inherited this trust, located and invested with the mantle the Sheikh Ahmed Faruqi of Sirhind.

This Naqshbandi teacher had already been initiated into sixteen Dervish Orders by his father, who had sought and reconstructed the scattered lore of Sufism in extensive and perilous journeys.

It is believed that Sirhand was the place designated for the appearance of the Great Teacher, and a succession of saints has awaited his manifestation for generations.

As a consequence of the appearance of Faruqi and his acceptance by the chiefs of all the Orders of the time, the Naqshbandis now initiate disciples into all of the four major streams of Sufism: the Christi, Qadiri, Suhrawardi and Nasqshbandi Ways.

"The Lame Man and the Blind Man" is ascribed to Sheikh Ahmed Faruqi, who died in 1615. It is supposed to be read only after receiving definite instructions to do so: or by those who have already studied Hakim Sanai's "Blind Ones and the Matter of the Elephant."[9]

THE LAME MAN AND THE BLIND MAN

A lame man walked into a Serai ("Inn") one day, and sat down beside a figure already seated there. "I shall never be able to reach the Sultan's banquet," he sighed, "because, due to my infirmity, I am unable to move fast enough."

The other man raised his head. "I, too have been invited," he said, "But my plight is worse than yours. I am blind, and cannot see the road, although I have also been invited."

A third man who heard them talking said: "But, if you only realized it, you two would have between you the means to reach your destination. The blind man can walk, with the lame one on his back. You can use the feet of the blind man and the eyes of the lame to direct you."

Thus the two were able to reach the end of the road, where the feast awaited them.

But on their way, they stopped to rest at another Serai. They explained their condition to two other men who were sitting

[9]Ibid., pp. 209–10.

disconsolately there. Of these two, one was deaf and the other
dumb. They had both been invited to the feast. The dumb one
had heard but was unable to explain to his friend the deaf
man. The deaf man could talk but had nothing to say.

Neither of them arrived at the feast; for this time there was no
third man to explain to them that there was a difficulty, let
alone how they might resolve it.[10]

We are all the people in this story. If we are blind (percep-
tually myopic) or lame (limited in our ability to get things done), at
least we have a chance with the help of a wiser one (the "third
man" in the story). But if we are deaf (think we know and won't
listen) or dumb (don't want to know), then we haven't a chance.
Many Sufi stories are also nonlinear in nature.

PARADISE OF SONG

Ahangar was a mighty swordsmith who lived in one of
Afghanistan's remote eastern valleys. In time of peace he
made steel ploughs, shoed horses and, above all, he sang.

The songs of Ahangar, who is known by different names in
various parts of Central Asia, were eagerly listened to by the
people of the valleys. They came from the forests of giant
walnut trees, from the snowcapped Hindu-Kush, from
Qataghan and Badakhshan, from Khanabad and Kunar, from
Herat and Paghman, to hear his songs.

Above all, the people came to hear the song of all songs,
which was Ahangar's Song of the Valley of Paradise.

This song had a haunting quality, and a strange lilt, and most
of all it had a story which was so strange that people felt they
knew the remote Valley of Paradise of which the smith sang.
Often they asked him to sing it when he was not in the mood
to do so, and he would refuse. Sometimes people asked him
whether the Valley was truly real, and Ahangar could only say:

"The Valley of the Song is as real as real can be."

"But how do you know?" the people would ask, "Have you
ever been there?"

"Not in any ordinary way," said Ahangar.

[10]Ibid., p. 209.

To Ahangar, and to nearly all the people who heard him, the Valley of the Song was, however, real, real as real can be.

Aisha, a local maiden whom he loved, doubted whether there was such a place. So, too, did Hasan, a braggart and fearsome swordsman who swore to marry Aisha, and who lost no opportunity of laughing at the smith.

One day, when the villagers were sitting around silently after Ahangar had been telling his tale to them, Hasan spoke:

"If you believe that this valley is so real, and that it is, as you say, in those mountains of Sangan yonder, where the blue haze rises, why do you not try to find it?"

"It would not be right, I know that," said Ahangar.

"You know what it is convenient to know, and do not know what you do not want to know!" shouted Hasan. "Now, my friend, I propose a test. You love Aisha, but she does not trust you. She has no faith in this absurd Valley of yours. You could never marry her, because when there is no confidence between man and wife, they are not happy and all manner of evils result."

"Do you expect me to go to the valley, then?" asked Ahangar.

"Yes," said Hasan and all the audience together.

"If I go and return safely, will Aisha consent to marry me?" asked Ahangar.

"Yes," murmured Aisha.

So Ahangar, collecting some dried mulberries and a scrap of bread, set off for the distant mountains.

He climbed and climbed, until he came to a wall which encircled the entire range. When he had ascended its sheer sides, there was another wall, even more precipitous then the first. After that there was a third, then a fourth, and finally a fifth wall.

Descending on the other side, Ahangar found that he was in a valley, strikingly similar to his own.

People came out to welcome him, and as he saw them, Ahangar realized that something very strange was happening.

Months later, Ahangar the Smith, walking like an old man, limped into his native village, and made for his humble hut.

As word of his return spread throughout the countryside, people gathered in front of his home to hear what his adventures had been.

Hasan the swordsman spoke for them all, and called Ahangar to his window.

There was a gasp as everyone saw how old he had become.

"Well, Master Ahangar, and did you reach the Valley of Paradise?"

"I did."

"And what was it like?"

Ahangar, fumbling for his words, looked at the assembled people with a weariness and hopelessness that he had never felt before. He said:

"I climbed and I climbed, and I climbed. When it seemed as though there could be no human habitation in such a desolate place, and after many trials and disappointments, I came upon a valley. This valley was exactly like the one in which we live. And then I saw the people. Those people are not only like us people: they are *the same people*. For every Hasan, every Aisha, every Ahangar, every anybody whom we have here, there is another one, exactly the same in that valley."

"These are likenesses and reflections to us, when we see such things. But it is we who are the likeness and reflections of them—we who are here, we are their twins..."

Everyone thought that Ahangar had gone mad through his privations, and Aisha married Hasan the swordsman. Ahangar rapidly grew old and died. And all the people, every one who had heard this story from the lips of Ahangar, first lost heart in their lives, then grew old and died, for they felt that something was going to happen over which they had no control and from which they had no hope, and so they lost interest in life itself.

It is only once in a thousand years that this secret is seen by man. When he sees it, he is changed. When he tells its bare facts to others, they wither and die out.

People think that such an event is a catastrophe, and so they must not know about it, for they cannot understand (such is the nature of their ordinary life) that they have more selves than one, more hopes than one, more chance than one—up there, in the Paradise of the Song of Ahangar, the mighty smith.[11]

Like the use of lateral thinking, the nonlinear, parabolic feature of Sufi stories can assist you in using your mind in an unfamiliar, unpatterned way. If you find it difficult to relate to some of the stories, this may be part of the reason. Many have bought Shah's books, read some stories and found them incomprehensible or even uninteresting. But the brain needs exercise or it will become sluggish.

The teaching stories, or "oral literature," as they are referred to, are an outstanding feature of Shah's works. Teaching stories are similar in appearance to Aesopean fables or fairy tales, and they entertain as well. Many also have an overt moral to them; but the similarities stop there. Sufi teaching tales, of ancient or modern origin, are best described as technical devices especially designed to penetrate into the deepest levels of the mind, to affect areas of the brain inaccessible in any other way. Unlike any other form of literature, the tales not only say something, they *do* something.

The tales also have several layers of meaning. These meanings are revealed to the reader at various points in his or her progression through life. The stories provoke the mind, shock, and stimulate—sometimes in ways that are not immediately noticed. The results or effects may not be felt for hours, weeks, or even years. Sometimes one must undergo certain experiences in his or her life before certain meanings in the stories reveal themselves (the deepest layers of meaning are usually unlocked with the assistance of a guide, within a broader, prescribed course of study). Like the Rorshach ink-blot test, the stories can affect different people in totally different ways—evoking mental impressions or interpretations of kaleidoscopic multiplicity.

The tales can also have a "mirroring" effect in that they will activate reactions or attitudes for the reader to self-examine; they force you to take a good look at yourself.

Many of the Sufi fables are presented as jokes and these are typified in the Mulla Nasrudin stories. Nasrudin is the Everyman

[11]Idries Shah, "Paradise of Song," *The Wisdom of the Idiots* (New York: Dutton, 1969), pp. 77–80.

of the Arab world—at once, both the wise man and the fool. "The Mulla is variously referred to as stupid, improperly clever, the possessor of mystical secrets. The dervishes use him as a figure to illustrate, in their teachings, the antics and characteristics of the human mind."[12]

While Nasrudin stories may be told as jokes (Nasrudin jokes are very popular in Asia and the Near East), their real purpose is to present an impact to our minds—to break patterns, and to provide illumination.

NEVER KNOW WHEN IT MIGHT
COME IN USEFUL

Nasrudin sometimes took people for trips in his boat. One day a fussy pedagogue hired him to ferry him across a very wide river.

As soon as they were afloat the scholar asked whether it was going to be rough.

"Don't ask me nothing about it," said Nasrudin.

"Have you never studied grammar?"

"No," said the Mulla.

"In that case, half your life has been wasted."

The Mulla said nothing.

Soon a terrible storm blew up. The Mulla's crazy cockleshell was filling with water.

He leaned over towards his companion.

"Have you ever learnt to swim?"

"No," said the pendant.

"In that case, schoolmaster, all your life is lost, for we are sinking."[13]

Although amusing to some, and conveying a moral to others, this "joke" is actually a multifaceted commentary all at once: about the limits of conventional education, the purpose of life, how our

[12]Idries Shah, *The Exploits of the Incomparable Mulla Nasrudin* (New York: Dutton, 1972), p. 9.
[13]Ibid., p. 18.

obsessions can trap us (and destroy us), how a seemingly impoverished, uneducated person can be advanced (by another scale of judgement), and why we need to be prepared in order to arrive at our ultimate destination.

In his book, *The Mechanism of Mind*, Edward de Bono noted that in humor "there is a sudden switchover from one way of looking at things to another. This is exactly similar to the insight process."[14] He also notes that humor (and insight) involves the breaking of expectations and patterns—a lubricant for the brain.

And according to Idries Shah, "As a shock-applier and tension-releaser and an indicator of false situations, humor, certainly to the Sufi in traditional usage, is one of the most effective instruments and diagnostic aids ... How a person reacts to a joke will also tell us, and possibly him or her, what his or her blocks and assumptions have been, and can help dissolve them, to everyone's advantage."[15]

In his introduction to the recently reprinted Sufi classic, *The Secret Garden*, by the thirteenth century Persian sage Mahmud Shabistari, Shiekh Imdad Hussein *el Qadiri* notes,

> Sufism has thrown off its Oriental and Cultist accretions. Only those who want primitive thought are unlikely to be able to welcome back into the fold a science which offers, as a sociological journal [New Society] put it, "real possibilities and practical alternatives to our present ways of operating ... relevant, fruitful and urgent for our present society."[16]

He then points out that "the present work, *The Secret Garden* of Shabistari can, if read from the point of view of psychology and current social problems, give valuable pointers for personal action."[17] And, although written from within the culture of Central Asia in the Middle Ages, "It also illustrates the expression of eternal truths and exercises of various kinds."[18]

[14] Edward de Bono, *The Mechanism of Mind* (New York: Simon & Schuster, 1969), p. 171.
[15] Idries Shah, *Special Illumination* (London: Octagon Press, 1977), p. 7.
[16] Mahmud Shabistari: (translated by Johnson Pasha), *The Secret Garden* (London: Octagon Press, 1969), p. 17. The Introduction by el-Quadiri is also reprinted in Leonard Lewin's ed., *The Elephant in the Dark* (New York: Dutton, 1972), pp. 137–43.
[17] Ibid., p. 17.
[18] Pat Williams, "Teaching Stories," *New Society*, 1, no. 299 (June 20, 1968), p. 20.

As a further example of the Sufi phenomenon of timelessness and contemporary relevance, Idries Shah's book, *Caravan of Dreams* provides us with a collection of meditations by Jalaludin Rumi, a mystic and poet of the fourteenth century.

Dr. Robert Ornstein notes in his book, *The Nature of Human Consciousness*, these " 'meditations by Rumi' are intended as material for thought, ideas to be turned over in the mind."

MEDITATIONS OF RUMI

There is no cause for fear. It is imagination, blocking you as a wooden bolt holds the door. Burn that bar ...

Every thought has a parallel action.

Every prayer has a sound and a physical form.

The man of God is not an expert made by books.

First you were mineral, then vegetable, then man. You will be an angel, and you will pass beyond that, too.

There are a thousand forms of mind.

Counterfeiters exist because there is such a thing as real gold.

Whoever says everything is true is a fool, whoever says all is untrue is a liar.

A great obstacle in the Path is fame.

God's mirror: the front is the heart, its back the world.

The infinite universe lies beyond this world.

They say: "He cannot be found"... Something that cannot be "found" is what I desire.

To make wine, you must ferment the grape juice.

Water does not run uphill.

You have two "heads." The orginal, which is concealed, the derivative, which is the visible one.

The moment you entered this world of form, an escape ladder was put out for you.

Wool only becomes a carpet because knowledge is available.

To boil water you need an intermediary—the vessel.

If the sea-water did not rise into the sky, where would the garden get its life?

A totally wise man would cease to exist in the ordinary sense.

You make no spark by striking earth on a flint.

The worker is hidden in the workshop.

To the ignorant, a pearl seems a mere stone.

If a tree could move on foot or feather, it would not suffer the agony of the saw nor the wounds of the blade.

What bread looks like depends upon whether you are hungry or not.

You may seek a furnace, but it would burn you. Perhaps you need only the weaker flame of a lamp.[18]

The value of Shah's materials is best appreciated when looked at as a totality. All twenty-five of his books published in the last fifteen years comprise a broad spectrum of interrelated studies. He has provided us with a rich diversity of modalities. The experiential effects of these materials are equally as diverse: laughter, amusement, beauty, entertainment, insight, perception, and learning. The materials as a whole cannot be categorized or classified so the system is also a nonsystem.

The objective of Shah's materials (and Sufism as well) is unlike most other forms of instruction. Their purpose is not to indoctrinate or provide a body of thought to which one is expected to accept or reject. Neither are the materials to be too carefully analyzed or used for scholarly, comparative purposes. Rather, their aim is simply to provoke experience—to juggle the brain out of its customary ruts and to attune the mind to new possibilities.

[18]Idries Shah, *Caravan of Dreams* (New York: Viking/Penguin, 1972), pp. 79–80.

chapter fourteen
HUMAN NATURE

One day a man reproached Bayazid, the great mystic of the ninth century, saying that he had fasted and prayed and so on for thirty years and had not found the joy which Bayazid described. Bayazid told him that he might continue for three hundred years and still not find it.

"How is that?" asked the would-be illuminate.

"Because your vanity is a barrier to you."

"Tell me the remedy."

"The remedy is one which you cannot take."

"Tell me, nevertheless."

Bayazid said: "You must go to the barber and have your (respectable) beard shaved. Remove all your clothes and put a girdle around yourself. Fill a nosebag with walnuts and suspend it from your neck. Go to the market-place and call out: 'A walnut will I give to any boy who will strike me on the back of the neck.' Then continue on to the justices' session so that they may see you."

"But I cannot do that; please tell me something else that would do as well."

"This is the first move, and the only one," said Bayazid, but I

126

had already told you that you would not do it; so you cannot be cured.[1]

Idries Shah offers this commentary:

El-Ghazali, in his *Alchemy of Happiness* seeks with this parable to emphasize his repeated argument that some people, however sincere in seeking truth they may appear to themselves or even to other people—may in fact be motivated by vanity or self-seeking which imposes a complete barrier to their learning.[2]

Psychologist Abraham Maslow noted five levels of needs in the human being: physiological, safety, love, esteem, and self-actualization. As one need becomes satisfied, the next takes over. Maslow pointed out, however, that few reach the final and ultimate level of self-actualization; for most people, self-esteem represents the peak of their development. Particularly in this "me" generation, we admire those who can say, "Hey, I *really* like myself!"

While self-esteem might be a quality valued by various cultures (particularly in Southern California), and is often the goal psychologists set for their patients, it is also something that limits the expression of one's full mental potential. In other words, now that we like ourselves, what are we going to *do* about it?

EVERY LITTLE HELPS

Nasrudin loaded his ass with wood for the fire, and instead of sitting in the saddle, sat astride one of the logs.

"Why don't you sit in the saddle?" someone asked.

"What! And add my weight to what the poor animal has to carry? My weight is on the *wood*, and it is going to stay there."[3]

Now there's some self-esteem. Nasrudin *likes* himself because he *thinks* he's helping the ass.

[1]Idries Shah, "Bayazid and the Selfish Man," *Tales of the Dervishes* (New York: Dutton, 1970), p. 180.
[2]Ibid., p. 180.
[3]Idries Shah, "Every Little Helps," *The Exploits of the Incomparable Mulla Nasrudin* (New York: Dutton, 1972), p. 81.

FIXED IDEAS

"How old are you, Mulla?"

"Forty."

"But you said the same last time I asked you, two years ago!"

"Yes, I always stand by what I have said."[4]

And there is some pride. Self-esteem coupled with pride breeds dogmatism. Dogmatism, or the penchant for being right, blocks our ability to learn. Once we can no longer learn, our brains become frozen and all personal progress ceases.

Self-esteem and pride, at their extremes, have been described by the science fiction writer, A.E. Van Vogt, and characterized in his book, *The Violent Man.* Van Vogt spent several years studying "the violent male" or "the right man" and offers some valuable insights.

It was in the 1950s that Van Vogt became interested in what would now be called "male chauvinist piggery," and began to study examples of it in divorce cases. He observed that there is a type of man who demands one code of conduct for himself and another for his wife. And it dawned on him that he had stumbled on an aspect of human nature that had been overlooked by orthodox psychology.

The chief characteristic of this type of male was an obsession with being right. Under no circumstances would he ever admit that he might be wrong. If something upset him, he would tend to look for somebody to blame and pour his irritation on the head of the nearest person, particularly if it happened to be a member of his own family. He could never admit that he might be to blame. With strangers, or colleagues at work, he would usually seem to be a perfectly reasonable human being. Where his family was concerned, he was a kind of miniature Hitler. He was prone to pathological jealousy and could behave like the most puritanical of Victorian fathers. Yet he was often a philanderer and a seducer; sexual conquest was one of his most important sources of self-esteem. He made a habit of indulging every emotion without regard to the rights or wrongs of the matter. If contradicted, he was likely to

[4]Idries Shah, *The Pleasantries of the Incredible Mulla Nasrudin* (New York: Dutton, 1971), p. 38.

become violent. Van Vogt labelled him "the Right Man," or the Violent Male ...

... Anyone who has ever lived in a house with a Violent Male (or a Violent Female, for that matter) knows that it can be a long-drawn-out tragedy, a ruthless attempt to force other people into one's own mental moulds. All human beings have a tendency to daydream, to indulge in fantasies that flatter the ego. The Right Man tries to act out his fantasies and uses his authority to force others to support the charade. If, as occasionally happens, he manages to achieve a position of authority, he is likely to become utterly corrupted by self-indulgence, like so many tyrants and dictators of history. He can now indulge his fantasy of being omnipotent; he regards anyone who opposes his will as a criminal who deserves to suffer. Stalin and Hitler were Right Men; so, probably was Mao Tse Tung. When, shortly before Mao's death, the Chinese demonstrated in the Square of Heavenly Peace in Peking against the downfall of the moderate Teng Hsiao-Ping, many were arrested; these were all shot or sentenced to long terms in prison. Mao was old and sick but he could still be roused to murderous rage by the least sign of contradiction or opposition ...

It is when we begin to grasp its implications that this insight becomes truly alarming. Freud made us recognise that sex plays a far greater role in human life than Victorians cared to acknowledge (although it now seems clear that he carried it to the point of absurdity). Van Vogt's achievement is equally striking; he has shown that egoism can produce a form of mild insanity, and that we all suffer from this to some extent. This immediately undermines one of our basic assumptions about human nature: that men can be relied on to behave sensibly out of "rational self-interest." Rightness overrules self-interest; it can make a man blind to his own destruction provided he can inflict damage on his enemy—or, better still, make him beg for mercy. And we are living in a society where practically everyone suffers from some degree of "Rightness." Good manners and social conventions have been developed to minimise the friction. But whenever these fail, the conflict comes out into the open. Governments issue ultimatums and threaten war, and whole nations are willing to agree that a few million dead is a small price to pay for avenging an insult.[5]

[5]Colin Wilson, *Mysteries* (New York: Putnam's, 1978), pp. 181–86.

Although these are extreme cases, they are exaggerations of processes inherent in *all* of us—male or female. They are exaggerations of the king and queen in all of us; the dog or donkey who is stubborn, hates to be proven wrong, thinks he or she knows more than he or she really does, is rigid, intolerant, and proud. In other words, the authoritarian father-figure in everyone—the ruler of his territory.

The central point is that we must give up this "Mr." or "Ms. Right" attitude in order to further ourselves. It stands in our way of learning; it makes us repeat behavior patterns over and over.

Everything we learn or are trained to do merely relates to our survival on this planet. We learn how to work (vocational training), how to get by in school (education), how to get along with others (socialization training), how to live within the law (ethical and moral training), to have a family (reproduction), and so on. This "learning to get by" is sufficient for survival, but it only involves one-fifth of our brain power. The other four-fifths are closed off so that we can survive ("maintain").

If we wish to learn more, to learn anew, to break through, we need to reconsider ourselves. Mr. or Ms. Right must go. That's the first step. With today's society changing as fast as it is, we must discard the lurking male penchant for dominance.

Dr. Edward de Bono wrote a brilliant book, *The Greatest Thinkers: The Thirty Minds That Shaped Our Civilization* (New York: G. P. Putnam's Sons, 1976). Interestingly enough, all thirty minds were male (Moses, Confucius, Jesus, Descartes, Darwin, Freud, and so on). Why weren't there any females? Studies have proven males and females are equal in intelligence and both use about one-fifth of their brain—but why not women? Better to ask what prevented women from using more than their allotted one-fifth. The answer is quite simple, until just recently, we have existed in a Right Man-oriented civilization. And throughout the ages, women were too busy fighting off the attacks of crazed pillagers and plunderers, saving their children from the ravages of the bubonic plague, not to mention having time to throw a few potatoes and rabbits in a pot of hot water. How could they be expected to sit around and come up with the theory of relativity in their leisure time? But now that the roles are becoming redefined, the sands are beginning to shift.

THE POWER OF WOMEN

"Women hold up half the sky," says a Chinese proverb. Women represent the greatest single force for political renewal in a civilization thoroughly out of balance. Just as individuals are enriched by developing both the masculine and feminine sides of the self (independence and nurturance, intellect and intuition), so the society is benefiting from a change in the balance of power between the sexes.

The power of women is the powder keg of our time. As women enlarge their influence in policymaking and government, their *yin* perspective will push out the boundaries of the old *yang* paradigm. Women are neurologically more flexible than men, and they have had cultural permission to be more intuitive, sensitive, feeling. Their natural milieu has been complexity, change, nurturance, affiliation, a more fluid sense of time ...

In 1916 psychologist George Stratton of the University of Southern California was describing the inherent superiority of female brains in seeing the whole. Writing on "Feminism and Psychology" in *Century Magazine*, he expressed the hope that women would dispel masculine illusions when they took their rightful place in society. Men, he said, tend to fix on cogs instead of flesh and blood. Beginning with a generous wonder at nature, they end up with a fascination for the tool—the scientific instrument. They establish governments to give order to life, then end up coveting the functions of government more than life. "The masculine genius for organization," Stratton said, "needs women's sense of the heart of things, not the trappings."

Recently a woman psychologist suggested that human survival may require that the private virtues of women go public. "Perhaps the women's movement is part of an evolutionary process that will keep us from going the way of the dinosaur and the dodo."[6]

As Right Man chauvinism declines, as women give themselves freedom, as they become more liberated socially, so their *minds* will become liberated. de Bono's book spans 2,000 years; 500 years from now de Bono's *The Greatest Thinkers* will undoubtedly contain women.

[6]Marilyn Ferguson, *The Aquarian Conspiracy* (Los Angeles: J. P. Tarcher, 1980), pp. 226–28.

132 Human Nature

What are the qualities of a genius? Put one way, a genius and the Right Man are diametrically opposed.

In his studies of creativity and genius, Arthur Koestler notes,

> Only geniuses preserve their infantile voracity for "because"—and the naive hope that there *are* real answers to every question. "Why is the moon round? Why does the apple fall from the tree? Why are there five planets instead of twenty, and why do they move as they do? Why does milk go sour? Why could the dairymaid not get the pox? Why is the colour of a sailor's blood in the tropics a brighter red than in Hamburg? Why did the dead frog's leg twitch?" One of the hallmarks of genius is that he has never lost the habit of asking foolish questions like these—each of which led to a momentous discovery.[7]

How can anyone ever get a blinding flash of insight when they're preoccupied with always being right?

In an article titled "Some Assumptions of Orthodox Western Psychology," psychologist Charles Tart questions the assumption that knowledge or understanding is possible merely by collecting and processing information (if that were true, most scientific discoveries might never have been made). By looking to the wisdom of the ancient East, he recognizes that very likely, learning-beyond-the-norm may only come about by work within oneself—one's basic nature, emotions, personality, and so on, by self-development. In terms of an analogy—a mirror reflecting reality—we need to polish the rust from our mirrors first.

Assumption: We can understand the physical universe without understanding ourselves.

Physicists are not required to take courses in psychology or self-awareness as part of their training to become physicists.* They are studying the "outside" physical world, using their instruments and their intellects, and their own personalities and spiritual natures are not taken into consideration. To put it extremely, a first-class physicist making excellent progress in the physical sciences may torture children for a hobby. It is unlikely to affect his progress as a physicist unless he lets his

[7] Arthur Koestler, *The Act of Creation* (New York: The Sterling Lord Agency, 1964), p. 705.

emotions "interfere" with his work. The individual investigator's personality, as long as it is not so neurotic as to interfere with the application of his intellect to his work, is not considered particularly relevant in doing scientific work.

Many of the spiritual psychologies assume, to the contrary, that one's nature, one's personality, or one's level of spiritual being will have a profound effect on his understanding of the universe. Many of them suggest that one's level of being, if low, will not only affect his cognitive processes and so systematically distort the way he sees the universe and restrict his intellectual formulations, but may further react on the universe itself, thus giving a kind of false validation to his view. This is easy to see in, say, the social sciences. If you believe that men are inherently selfish because you are inherently selfish, it is easy to observe selfish behavior among the vast panorama of human activity and confirm your view. This confirmation may be a useful contribution to scientific knowledge insofar as you collect good observations and come up with hypotheses to explain various forms of that selfish behavior. That is as far as one would take that view as long as one assumes that the universe is basically dead. But if the universe is in some way alive and responsive, then your own level of being may affect not only your perceptions, evaluations, and ways of interacting with your fellow men, it may also have direct effects on the physical universe about you.

*[In a footnote to his first sentence, Tart notes:]

For that matter, orthodox, Western psychologists are almost never required to take any courses in self-awareness as part of their training.[8]

El-Ghazali, the 12th-century Persian sage wrote:

A camel is stronger than a man; an elephant is larger; a lion has greater valour; cattle eat more than man; birds are more virile. Man was made for the purpose of learning.[9]

But Ghazali was wise. He knew that learning is not conditioning, indoctrination, opinion-mouthing, and merely responding to

[8]Charles Tart, "Some Assumptions of Orthodox Western Psychology," *Transpersonal Psychologies* (New York: Harper & Row, Pub., 1975), p. 69.
[9]Idries Shah, *The Way of the Sufi* (New York: Dutton, 1970), p. 57.

stimulus. Learning, he noted, is akin to knowledge. It is under-standing, perception, and wisdom.

> There are many degrees of knowledge. The mere physical man is like the ant crawling on paper, who observes black lettering and attributes its production to the pen and to nothing more.[10]

Because of this flaw in our nature—our general lack of knowing how to learn—we carry this defect beyond ourselves and our relationships with others to a global scale.

The eminent historian and twice Pulitzer Prize winner, Barbara W. Tuchman, in a recent article begins by asking:

> A problem that strikes one in the study of history, regardless of period, is why man makes a poorer performance of government than of almost any other human activity. In this sphere, wisdom—meaning judgment acting on experience, common sense, available knowledge, and a decent appreciation of probability—is less operative and more frustrated than it should be. Why do men in high office so often act contrary to the way that reason points and enlightened self-interest suggests? Why does intelligent mental process so often seem to be paralyzed?

After presenting numerous historical examples, past and present, Tuchman answers her own question:

> Wooden-headedness is a factor that plays a remarkably large role in government. Wooden-headedness consists of assessing a situation in terms of preconceived fixed notions while ignoring or rejecting any contrary signs. It is acting according to wish while not allowing oneself to be confused by the facts.

The solution? Not easy, she says:

> Under the circumstances, what are the chances of improving the conduct of government? The idea of a class of professionals trained for the task has been around ever since Plato's *Republic* ...

[10]El-Ghazali, quoted by, Idries Shah, *The Sufis* (New York: Doubleday/Anchor, 1971), p. 177.

I do not know if the prognosis is hopeful or, given the underlying emotional drives, whether professionalism is the cure. In the Age of Enlightenment, John Locke thought the emotions should be controlled by intellectual judgment and that it was the distinction and glory of man to be able to control them. As witnesses of the twentieth century's record, comparable to the worst in history, we have less confidence in our species. Although professionalism can help, I tend to think that fitness of character is what government chiefly requires. How that can be discovered, encouraged, and brought into office is the problem that besets us."

It is said we have wars because wars have always occurred due to human nature. Crime continues to be a problem because it always has. Again, human nature. There will always be poor people and food shortages because of the rich and greedy—people, after all, have always been selfish and covetous.

But does this have to go on perpetually? If man was made for learning, does human nature need to be impervious to change? Does "human nature" reflect the one-fifth of our brains we use? Maybe our conception of human nature can change once we begin to use our heads; to use more than that one-fifth.

"Barbara W. Tuchman, "An Inquiry into the Persistence of Unwisdom in Government," *Esquire* (May 1980), pp. 25–31.

chapter fifteen
THE COMPLETE PERSON

The camel-driver has his plans; and the camel has his own
plans.
The organized mind can think well.
The Complete Man's mind can exist well.

—Rasul Shah[1]

The focus of this book has been on the brain—on ways to get better
use from that gray computer we carry around on our shoulders.

> But the brain clearly does not "explain" the mind. It may
> reveal how certain low-grade processes take place, or perhaps
> only *where* they take place, but it tells us nothing of the higher
> powers of consciousness—will, inspiration, creativity, intui-
> tion, humor, invention, moral choice.[2]

Science, because of its lab-coated physical-mechanistic model
of nature, deals with the brain and behavior, but has little to say
about the mind. Yet, the brain is a tool of the mind, and behavior is
an effect of the mind.

Why then, the concern with the mind? Because beyond the
brain is the mind and the person—our broader concern. It is the

[1]Idries Shah, "The Complete Man," *The Way of the Sufi* (New York: Dutton,
1970), p. 180.
[2]Theodore Roszak, *Person/Planet* (New York: Doubleday & Co., 1978), p. 56.

complete person who is well-integrated into that nebulous thing we call life; thus self-development must go even beyond learning how to develop one's brain.

So where do we go to learn about the whole person? About consciousness, and life itself? Test tubes and Bunsen burners provide only part of the answer. According to many contemporary thinkers, we need to look to the rich heritage of the East; to what are sometimes referred to as the ancient esoteric psychologies.

> In many ways as we consider the esoteric disciplines of Sufism, Buddhism, Yoga, they emerge as *sciences* of inner states, technologies developed to treat these most pressing problems of philosophy, psychiatry, psychology. Conventional science, as it is usually practiced often neglects the essential component in studying consciousness.[3]

In his books, *The Psychology of Consciousness* and *The Mind Field*, Dr. Robert Ornstein discusses the various disciplines of Eastern origin, with special emphasis upon the most influential of these disciplines—Sufism. He notes that while Sufism has its origins in the Near East and in ancient history, it continues to pervade our present civilization.

> A contemporary spiritual projection cannot demand either enslavement or a revival of guruism...the intent of a developed spiritual psychology is to provide a concentrated training in intuition perception. These terms and techniques have a specific meaning within the discipline of Sufism, and refer to experiential, not merely intellectual, understanding of many of the ultimate questions of philosophy and psychology.

> The methods of comtemporary Sufism are a means by which such understanding is brought about. The "knowledge" has at times been the province of philosophical, religious, esoteric, and occult systems. Many of the rituals and practices with which we are most familiar today are the remnants of those systems, diluted and reduced over time. Therefore, the first order of business is to distinguish past practices from current methodology. The "body of knowledge" that is Sufism has taken many forms, depending upon the culture and people

[3]Robert Ornstein, *The Nature of Human Consciousness* (New York: W.H. Freeman, 1973), p. 5.

who conspire it. It has existed within Hindu, Zoroastrian, Jewish, Christian, and non-religious frameworks. It is, of course, best known in the West as a development of Classical Islam. Proficiency in Islamic studies is not, however, a requirement for the understanding of Sufism.[4]

The anciently derived, esoteric, psycho-spiritual systems deal with all aspects of life and the person—the brain, mind, self, society, cultures, and the universe. They are best understood within an evolutionary framework, with a fundamental goal being the development of the complete person.

UNAWARE

You know nothing of yourself here and in this state.
    You are like the wax in the honeycomb: What
does it know of fire or guttering?
    When it gets to the stage of the waxen candle
and when light is emitted, then it knows.
    Similarly, you will know that when you were alive,
you were dead, and only thought yourself alive.[5]

—Attar of Nishapur

Various contemporary writers have noticed this death-like state of people (similar to the state one assumes while riding the subways of New York), attributing it to cultural conditioning and a machine-like existence. Joseph Chilton Pearce refers to this as being trapped in a "cosmic egg" and attempts to describe the possibility of breakthrough in his *Exploring the Crack in the Cosmic Egg*. For Pearce, "cracks" are ways out, but at best, these are described as momentary, bizarre experiences, the kind that only occur on rare occasions in our entire lifetime. He also notes, quite rightly, that even when people recognize their plight and believe they are rebelling for a cause, most attempted escapes are merely illusions. He refers to this as "the ace-up-the-sleeve" syndrome.

The church disintegrates as a buffer system, and hordes of eager replacements scrabble to fill the vacuum. Last year's

[4]Robert Ornstein, *The Mind Field* (New York: Simon & Schuster/Pocket Books, 1978), pp. 138–39.
[5]Idries Shah, "Unaware," *The Way of the Sufi* (New York: Dutton, 1970), p. 73.

drug scene fades to biofeedback feeding alpha waves to mind-control prophets riding the circuit with acupuncturists and high-energy mental states-through-protein-intake-boys making way for electronic human biocomputed data-feeding mind-zapping behind the Iron Curtain secrets of ESP, black magic, ooh-ah chemistry-clowns with astral travel and god-in-the-pill, the test tube, the sleep-learning machine, and LSD in the cosmic tank while the Swami-of-the-Month-Club jets this year's Savior fresh from India......

After each go-round, when the dust settles, it appears that something was missing ... but wait—dig the latest from Calcutta, and off we go—to the newest psychic fix parley, the Chataqua Circuit risen from the dead.[6]

We all seem to know someone who started out dropping acid in the sixties, then graduated to *est*, Scientology, and self-actualization retreats. However, even those of us who consider bowling with the neighbors as a *really* wild time, have our form of escapes; escapes which are more acceptable than running away to an encounter-group weekend.

The ace-up-the-sleeve syndrome can never be exhausted. The housewife shopping for trinkets, stuffing her overstuffed house with more junk, envying her neighbor's larger house and greater piles of junk; nagging her husband to "buy up" in the world and get out of this dump; stuffing her overstuffed body with junk ... and eyeing the telly for laughs only to eye the new round of trinkets and junk ... [7]

As the wheel turns, the squirrel scrambles around in its cage. It would bite off its tail to make a fur coat. The process never ends, never goes anywhere. There is always a new carrot at the end of a stick waiting for us, once we've chewed up the old one (if we're lucky enough to get that close).

And every culture has its carrots. In the jungles of Borneo, it's being a good hunter. In America it's the wealth-and-power syndrome, coupled with the finding-the-perfect-mate syndrome. In Japan, your cultural carrot is your company; you eat, breathe, and

[6]Joseph Chilton Pearce, *Exploring the Crack in the Cosmic Egg* (New York: Julian Press, 1974), p. 79.
[7]Ibid., pp. 79–80.

exercise for the corporation. In China, it's the state; if you can't do something glorious on behalf of the Revolution, go play in a rice paddy.

All of us have been successfully sold on our cultural carrots and few of us realize that we are under a spell.

> There is an Eastern tale which speaks about a very rich magician who had a great many sheep. But at the same time, this magician was very mean. He did not want to hire shepherds, nor did he want to erect a fence about the pasture where his sheep were grazing. The sheep consequently often wandered into the forest, fell into ravines, and so on, and above all they ran away, for they knew that the magician wanted their flesh and skins and this they did not like.

> At last the magician found a remedy. He *hypnotized* his sheep and suggested to them first of all that they were immortal and that no harm was being done to them when they were skinned, that, on the contrary, it would be very good for them and even pleasant; secondly he suggested that the magician was a *good master* who loved his flock so much that he was ready to do anything in the world for them; and in the third place he suggested to them that if anything at all were going to happen to them it was not going to happen just then, at any rate not that day, and *therefore* they had no need to think about it. Further the magician suggested to his sheep that they were not sheep at all; to some of them he suggested they were *lions*, to others that they were *eagles*, to others that they were men, and to others that they were *magicians*.

> And after this all his cares and worries about the sheep came to an end. They never ran away again, but quietly awaited the time when the magician would require their flesh and skins.

> This tale is a very good illustration of man's position.[8]

It's easy to baa around and be a sheep. But in order to escape this hypnotized sheep state, several things must happen. You must first become aware of your situation. Do a little wool-gathering, so to speak, since we are referring to our cloven-hoofed friends. Then, you must become thoroughly fed up with your

[8]P.D. Ouspensky, *In Search of the Miraculous* (New York: Harcourt Brace and Jovanovich, 1949), p. 219.

situation—hit rock bottom—the only way to go is up. However, most people stop here. They don't seem to realize that you can go up. They may be aware of their conditioning and *claim* they would like to get out of it, but they aren't willing to make the right efforts. This is the old ace-up-the-sleeve phenomenon and is simply a state of self-deception. When it comes right down to it, most people are so completely addicted to their customary way of life and thinking, that the thought of withdrawal (just like a junkie) alone is overwhelming.

ON ENTERING, LIVING IN—LEAVING—THE WORLD

Man, you enter the world reluctantly, crying, as a forlorn babe;
Man, you leave this life, deprived again, crying again, with regret.
Therefore live this life in such a way that none of it is really wasted.
You have to become accustomed to it after not having been accustomed to it.
When you have become accustomed to it, you will have to become used to being without it.
Meditate upon this contention.
Die, therefore, "before you die," in the words of the Purified One.
Complete the circle before it is completed for you.
Until you do, unless you have—then expect bitterness at the end as there was in the beginning; in the middle as there will be at the end.
You did not see the pattern as you entered; and when you entered—you saw another pattern.
When you saw this apparent pattern, you were prevented from seeing the threads of the coming pattern.
Until you see both, you will be without contentment—*Whom* do you blame? And *why* do you blame?[9]

—Hashim the Sidqi, on Rumi

How do you make the transfer from the apparent pattern to the real one? From your secondary self to your true self?

[9]Idries Shah, "On Entering ... ," *The Way of the Sufi* (New York: Dutton, 1970), p. 267.

Once you get past the ace-up-your-sleeve stage, you may wish to investigate the possibilities of a true teaching system. By this, of course, we aren't referring to schools, colleges, or universities that only serve the needs of the culture. The same can be said for a career in conventional science. Academic psychology can't help you (and they will be the first to admit it) nor can psychotherapy. Psychotherapy will only cure your ills, make you "normal"—psychotherapy is like taking a broken-down car and getting it in running condition. A true teaching system takes the apparently smooth-running car and gets it to fly.

GOOD AND BAD

There is no philosophical teacher nor system which will tell you to do other than good. You will probably be advised to strive against what is bad.

This is the first lesson, of course. But one should want to go beyond. The succeeding lessons are not taught by inflexible principle, nor by ordinary cultivation, nor by standardised exercises.

The succeeding lessons are all on what is good and what is bad, in the successive stages of a person's life; in the different epochs of a culture, in the various expressions of a teaching.

You can only learn this from the exponents of a contemporary school, rooted in the most ancient past, expressing this in institutions designed to be effective. These are not made for attraction-value nor for the robustness of the vehicle.[10]

Lucky is the seeker who can see through the dearth of false systems, bogus gurus, hucksters, and deceptive practices. But once one comes upon a legitimate teaching system, one's motives and approaches must be in correct alignment.

Besides insincerity, the most common mistake is for novices to (unknowingly) insist the conditions of study be on their terms. They may come into a study system with all sorts of preconceptions and expectations—a hidden agenda or mental model as to what they believe should be happening and what they should be doing in order to fulfill their goal. Novices *want* exercises when

[10]Idries Shah, *Reflections* (New York: Viking/Penguin, 1971), p. 78.

what they really need is information. They may wish to dance and sing when all they first need to do is read. Neophytes may want their teacher to give them more attention when they really need less. They may want study materials to be presented to them in a timely and orderly A-to-Z fashion whereas a nonsequential approach may be best. They might think they should be fasting, meditating, breathing a certain way; they may insist on celibacy, vegetarianism, or certain forms of exotic attire.

Once past this expectancy hurdle (which can sometimes take several years), the aspirant may then be ready to learn how to learn. Learning how to learn comes before actual higher development; on the principle that if you would like a beautiful garden you had better eliminate the weeds first.

Learning how to learn, or the long phase of preparative studies, is best done within a group setting—in the company of persons with similar long-term goals. Here, one learns about oneself and others and experiences a fore-taste of harmony.

PREPARATION

In order to digest food, a man needs a stomach. Who troubles himself to inquire, however, whether a would-be wise man is correspondingly well prepared?[11]

Following a phase of preparation (duration of the phase is not fixed: it depends on several factors, but normally takes several years), one is in a position to move forward. This requires as much of giving as receiving. In due time, with the right effort, right people, right materials, right guidance, one comes into a realm of experience unlike any other.

WHEN A MAN MEETS HIMSELF

One of man's greatest difficulties is also his most obvious drawback. It could be corrected if anyone troubled himself to point it out often and cogently enough.

It is the difficulty that man is describing himself when he thinks that he is describing others.

How often do you hear people say, about me:

[11]Ibid., p. 67.

"I regard this man as the Qutub (magnetic Pole) of the Age?"

He means, of course: "*I* regard this man..."

He is describing his own feelings or convictions, when what we might want to know is something about the person or thing being described.

When he says: "This teaching is sublime," he means: "This appears to suit me." But we might have wanted to know something about the teaching, not how he thinks it influences him.

Some people say: "But a thing can truly be known by its effect. Why not observe the effect upon a person?"

Most people do not understand that the effect of, say, sunlight on trees is something constant. In order to know the nature of the teaching, we would have to know the nature of the person upon whom it has acted. The ordinary person cannot know this: all he can know is what that person assumes to be an effect upon himself—and he has no coherent picture of what "himself" is. Since the outward observer knows even less than the person describing himself, we are left with quite useless evidence. We have no reliable witness.

Remember, that while this situation still obtains, there will generally be an equal number of people saying: "This is marvellous," as are saying: "This is ridiculous." This is ridiculous really means: "This appears ridiculous to me," and this is marvellous means: "This appears marvellous to me."

Do you really enjoy being like that?

Many people do, while energetically pretending otherwise.

Would you like to be able to test what really is ridiculous or marvellous, or anything in between?

You can do it, but not when you presume that you can do it without practice, without any training, in the midst of being quite uncertain as to what it is you are and why you like or dislike anything.

When you have found yourself you can have knowledge. Until then you can only have opinions. Opinions are based on habit and what you conceive to be convenient to you.

The study of the Way requires self-encounter along the way. You have not met yourself yet. The only advantage of meeting others in the meantime is that one of them may present you to yourself.

Before you do that, you will possibly imagine that you have met yourself many times. But the truth is that when you do meet yourself, you come into a permanent endowment and bequest of knowledge that is like no other experience on earth.[12]

—Tariqavi

Thus, the path toward becoming a complete person starts with realizing one's status, accepting it, and most importantly, opening up one's self to change. The total process of transformation may take an entire lifetime. Nobody said it was easy. But the efforts expended can "make all the difference in the world"—and in all your worlds to come.

[12]Idries Shah, *Wisdom of the Idiots* (New York: Dutton, 1969), pp. 121–23.

AFTERWORD

People have occasionally asked me, if they work at developing their brain, will they then become psychic—will they become telepathic, be able to project thoughts, read minds, become spiritual healers, and be capable of precognition?

My belief is that we all have these abilities latent within, but several factors will determine their emergence. I think we can begin with certain basic potentials, as dealt with in this book, such as thinking laterally, comprehensive perception, dream awareness, and intuition. Responsibility and maturity are important, too. I also believe that if we fixate or focus upon extrasensory or psychic abilities *as ends in themselves*, we are least likely to succeed. It appears as though these psychic, or PSI phenomena, as they are called, are intimations of something larger—the ongoing evolution of human consciousness itself. The final chapter of this book is probably the key to understanding the issue of higher abilities, where it is implied that we should focus upon development of our complete selves—that we may need specialized guidance in this respect, and that as the result of proper self-development, psychic abilities will manifest themselves spontaneously, as happy by-products, rather than as faculties to gloat over or make a fuss about. As I indicated in my earlier book, *Unstress Yourself: Strategies for Effective Stress Control* (Santa Barbara: Ross-Erikson Publishers,

1979). "Each one of us has within an essence—a potential seed waiting to be released." And while psychic abilities and blissful states of mind may accompany this unfoldment, "the prime objective is the search for truth, knowledge, reality, and the betterment of ourselves and humanity."

INDEX